# Fun & Fabulous
# Pillows to Sew

## 15 Easy Designs for the
## Complete Beginner

# Fun & Fabulous
# Pillows to Sew

## 15 Easy Designs for the Complete Beginner

*Valerie Van Arsdale Shrader*

LARK BOOKS

A Division of Sterling Publishing Co., Inc.
New York

ART DIRECTOR:
Stacey Budge

COVER DESIGNER:
Barbara Zaretsky

ASSOCIATE EDITOR:
Nathalie Mornu

ASSOCIATE ART DIRECTOR:
Shannon Yokeley

ART PRODUCTION ASSISTANT:
Jeff Hamilton

EDITORIAL ASSISTANCE:
Delores Gosnell

ILLUSTRATOR:
Susan McBride

PHOTOGRAPHER:
Stewart O'Shields

Library of Congress Cataloging-in-Publication Data

Shrader, Valerie Van Arsdale.
  Fun & fabulous pillows to sew : 15 easy designs for the
complete beginner / Valerie Van Arsdale Shrader. -- 1st ed.
      p. cm.
   Includes index.
   ISBN 1-57990-802-0 (hardcover)
 1. Pillows. 2. Machine sewing. I. Title. II. Title: Fun
and fabulous pillows to sew.
TT410.S37 2005
646.2'1--dc22

                                    2006012435


10 9 8 7 6 5 4 3 2 1

First Edition

Published by Lark Books, A Division of
Sterling Publishing Co., Inc.
387 Park Avenue South, New York, N.Y. 10016

Distributed in Canada by Sterling Publishing,
c/o Canadian Manda Group, 165 Dufferin Street
Toronto, Ontario, Canada M6K 3H6

Distributed in the United Kingdom by GMC Distribution Services,
Castle Place, 166 High Street, Lewes, East Sussex, England BN7 1XU

Distributed in Australia by Capricorn Link (Australia) Pty Ltd.,
P.O. Box 704, Windsor, NSW 2756 Australia

If you have questions or comments about this book, please contact:
Lark Books
67 Broadway
Asheville, NC 28801
(828) 253-0467

Manufactured in China

ISBN 13: 978-1-57990-802-7
ISBN 10: 1-57990-802-0

For information about custom editions, special sales, premium and corporate
purchases, please contact Sterling Special Sales Department at 800-805-5489 or
specialsales@sterlingpub.com.

# Contents

# Introduction

*Let's engage in a little pillow talk, shall we?*

Nothing can change the personality of a room, or a couch, or a bed, faster than a group of really cool pillows. Watch your sofa go from dull to dazzling by tossing on a couple of bright patchwork pillows, or add a sparkle to your boudoir with some beaded bolsters. Try it, you'll see! But since it's so easy to perform a quick face-lift, why aren't we doing it every time we get bored with our décor?

Let's examine this question for a moment. You've probably shopped for pillows at your favorite shop, or from your favorite catalog, but gasped at the price. Or perhaps you spotted a cute little bolster that you could afford, but the color wasn't quite right. If you lower your expectations and go budget shopping, it's the old you-get-what-you-pay-for syndrome—something cheaply made that's not exactly your dream pillow, in color, shape, or decoration. (You have *vision*, after all.)

I'm happy to announce that there's a solution to this problem, and it's creative and fun, too. Here it is—make your own fabulous pillows! Don't worry if you've neglected to learn how to sew, because I'm going to teach you how, right here in this book. If you've been, oh, intimidated by garment sewing, with the patterns and precise cutting and fitting, fear no more, because a pillow is the easiest little sewing project you can imagine. At its most basic, it's nothing more than two pieces of fabric stitched together with a few simple seams—you could practically do it in your sleep. You can brag to your friends about your newfound DIY skill, and you'll never have to settle for a size or a color that's not perfect.

I could go on and on about how pillows are the ideal thing to learn to sew. They don't take much fabric—about ½ yard at the

most—and the pillow is a fabulous canvas to explore. You can add just about any decorative element to a pillow—embroidery, elegant ribbon, funky trim, buttons, stitching, you name it. And because it's a small thing, you're not spending hours and hours of your precious time slaving away over the sewing machine. (And really, if you slave away over anything, it should involve romance.) In *Fun & Fabulous Pillows*, we're going to work our way through the entire process, from talking about fabric to learning basic sewing and embellishing techniques. We've got lots of great photos and illustrations to make the new (or reincarnated) sewer feel confident when she sits down at the machine. And wait until you see our pillow projects! There are 15 of the coolest designs you've ever seen, and some even offer variations on the basic theme. (We believe in giving you a bang for your buck.)

*Psst.* Here's a secret: sewing has been liberated. You don't have to finish the edges and turn everything under just so anymore. Contemporary techniques let the fabric do its own thing, and sometimes that means a raw edge that's raveling, or a seam that dares to expose itself on the right side of the fabric. Once you understand the basics, you can play around with the techniques. You have my permission. And you can take these basic concepts and use them to make garments, of course.

Back to the subject at hand, though. Since you can give a room a makeover with the addition of a few new pillows, why not do it? All you have to do is learn to sew, and once you see how easy it is, you probably won't want to stop. And of course, when you finally take a break, you'll have plenty of gorgeous pillows to rest your weary head on. Have I convinced you? Well, enough pillow chitchat, then. Let's get started.

# Guide to
# Making Fabulous Pillows

Where to begin? How about we discuss the different kinds of pillows? Just like dresses or skirts, there are different styles of pillows. The first step is deciding which kind you want to make.

## Pick a type

You're probably thinking, a pillow is a pillow. But there are actual types of pillows, with actual names such as a knife-edge pillow, a box-edge pillow, or a bolster. When you think about a "throw" pillow, you've probably got a knife-edge pillow in mind—it's the little square thing you toss onto the bed each morning after you get up. The strict definition of a knife-edge pillow is that it's a pillow that's a bit plump in the middle but skinny at the edges, while a box-edge pillow is the same thickness throughout. (A box-edge pillow can be square, rectangular, or round. Isn't that cool?) A bolster is a comfy cylinder that happens to fit just perfectly under your neck. There are variations of these three styles, too. For instance, there's a mock box that has the look of the more labor-intensive

FIGURE 1. Here are some common pillow styles. From left to right, they are: bolster, knife-edge, box-edge (square), box-edge (round), and mock box.

box-edge pillow, but the simplicity of the knife-edge pillow. Sounds good, huh?

And speaking of variations, there are many different ways to accent your pillow, and lots of different ways to open and close it, too, 'cause you've gotta be able to get the cozy stuffing inside. Let's spend a minute or two talking about that stuff that makes your pillow soft.

## Pick a pillow form

I'm sure you probably know that you can purchase a ready-made pillow form that you can just pop into your pillow after you've sewn it. Now, there's the economy version, stuffed with polyester fiberfill, and there's the luxury version, stuffed with feathers and down. I'll tell you honestly that the feather-filled pillow forms are really scrump-tious and make your pillow look a little more special. And they feel wonderful, too. But the polyester-filled pillow forms are perfectly adequate and very reasonably priced.

These stuffed pillow forms come in standard sizes and can be square, rectangular, round, or cylindrical (for a bolster).

You can use a variety of pillow forms and materials in your pillows, including foam, polyester fiberfill, and batting.

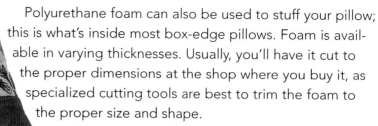

Polyurethane foam can also be used to stuff your pillow; this is what's inside most box-edge pillows. Foam is available in varying thicknesses. Usually, you'll have it cut to the proper dimensions at the shop where you buy it, as specialized cutting tools are best to trim the foam to the proper size and shape.

We've also used loose polyester fiberfill in several of our pillows. You can buy fiberfill in bags at fabric or craft stores. And you can use polyester batting to soften the edges of a foam pillow form, or you can create a form for a bolster with batting—simply roll it up to the proper thickness.

Now, how do you know which one of these forms you want to use in your pillow? Good question. Much of this decision boils down to personal taste. If you like your pillows sorta loose and floppy, stuff them with fiberfill, so you can control the amount of loft. This decision is also based on the type of pillow you make, though, as a box-edge pillow needs the structure of foam to achieve its perfect pillowness. We've used lots of different kinds of forms in this book, so look to our projects for some guidance on this subject.

For a luxurious pillow like this, consider using a form stuffed with feathers and down. Please!

## Choose a fabric

Well, our pillow talk is going quite well, don't you think? Let's turn our attention to the important subject of the fabric. I promise not to bore you to death with lots of information, but as a fabric junkie, I feel obligated to share some knowledge.

Fabrics can be woven or knit, and are made of fibers of various origins. Since you're interested in sewing, you probably already have a basic knowledge of the different types of fabric and what they're made from: the natural fibers, such as cotton, linen, wool, and silk; and the synthetic fibers, like polyester, acrylic, and nylon. (Isn't chemistry wonderful?) Rayon straddles these two categories, as it's synthesized from wood pulp; it's manmade, yet from a natural source. Other synthetic fabrics are made from petroleum products, and many fabrics are blends of natural and synthetic fibers.

Each bolt of fabric in the store will be labeled with its fiber content, its width, its price, and occasionally its laundering requirements. Now, the mention of the word "launder" brings up another important question about your pillow—is it just going to sit around and look good, or will you actually be using it? If your pillow is utilitarian and will get a lot of use, you'll probably need to launder it at some point. This decision directly relates to the kind of fabric that would be most appropriate for your pillow. Most silks, as you probably know, need to be professionally cleaned. So, do you want to be able to wash the pillow yourself, or are you willing to pay to have it dry-cleaned? Be sure to ask about laundering the fabric before you buy it, so you understand how you must care for your pillow after you've made it. Washable fabrics need to be preshrunk before being sewn, which simply means laundering them according to the manufacturer's recommendations before you start.

If a fabric is woven, its weave gives it specific characteristics. Satin, velvet, twill, and so on all describe the structure of the fabric and *not* its fiber content. Velvet can be made from silk, cotton, or polyester, for example. In any event, choose a fabric that's fairly tightly woven to retain the shape and fit of your pillow. For a happy sewing experience, consider using a cotton fabric for your first project because it handles and washes well, it's durable, and it's easy to sew.

When you're shopping for fabric, you've got two choices. You can look at a shop that specializes in dress-making goods, or you can visit a store that offers decorator fabrics for home décor applications. There are perfectly acceptable fabrics to be had at each type of shop. If you want a fussy little velvet pillow for pure decoration, look at a shop with garment fabrics. If you want a big cushion to toss on the floor, you're probably better off at a decorator shop. Decorator fabrics are designed for use in the home, so they can be very durable, and they are often wider than dressmaker's goods (more bang for the buck again).

Let your muse guide you as you select fabrics for your pillows. The set of pillows above uses three different fabrics, with varying weights and textures.

# Design your pillow

Now, the fun starts! Think about the kind of pillow you want to make, and let's plan it. (We're working our way to the sewing business, I promise. No need to rush.) Here's a little list of things to think about.

Shape

Size

Fabric

Pillow form

Closure

Okay. You've got a plain couch that needs some pizzazz. (Well, maybe a lot of pizzazz.) How about some knife-edge pillows? Let's make them a standard size so we can just pop a pillow form inside—let's say 14 x 14 inches. Now, how much fabric will you need to buy?

For most pillows, you need only about ½ yard of fabric (that's 18 inches for the math challenged), because the basic equation for making a pillow is that it should be 1 inch larger than the pillow form in each direction (width and length). If your pillow form is 14 x 14 inches, then you'll cut the pillow

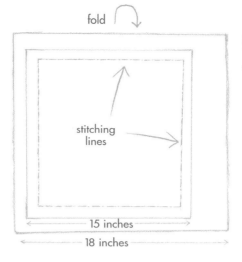

fold

stitching
lines

15 inches

18 inches

FIGURE 2. If you fold a ½ yard of fabric, you can cut out a pillow that fits a 14 x 14-inch form.

pieces to 15 x 15 inches. So, ½ yard of fabric is plenty, as you see in figure 2.

So, we need to pick out some amazing fabric to help out the poor ol' couch. These pillows are probably going to get a lot of wear, since they're in the living room. Let's go to the big decorator shop and look around—how about those cotton fabrics, one a stripe and the other a bold print, in complementary colors? Let's get ½ yard of each to make a set of pillows.

We're making progress, aren't we? Grab a couple of those stuffed polyester pillow forms and take everything home.

Hmmm. How are we going to close these pillows? Since we're going to need to wash the covers every so often, we want to make the pillow form easily removable. We could use a zipper, but for a first project, let's…not. A quick and easy way is to make a sham closing, so we can just slip the pillow form between the overlapping pieces on the back.

Great! We're done. We've decided how we want our pillows to look. Now we've got to learn to make them.

# Meet the
# Sewing Machine

The next step is to develop a meaningful relationship with your sewing machine, since it's the tool that allows you to make perfect pillows. Give it a friendly little pat and let's get to know it better. Later, when we Learn to Sew! on page 20, we'll discuss some of its functions in greater detail. I love my sewing machine! I really do.

## How it works

This fantastic invention creates a lockstitch when the thread from the needle (on top of the machine) and the thread from the bobbin (inside the machine) loop together in the fabric. This happens a gazillion times per minute when you sew. (Aren't you glad you don't have to do it by hand? I sure am.) That's the long, the short, and the zigzag of it.

Although machines share common characteristics, they vary by manufacturer. When I keep referring you to your own machine's manual, I'm not trying to ignore your needs; it's because there are some important yet subtle differences

It's fun to sew with great fabric!

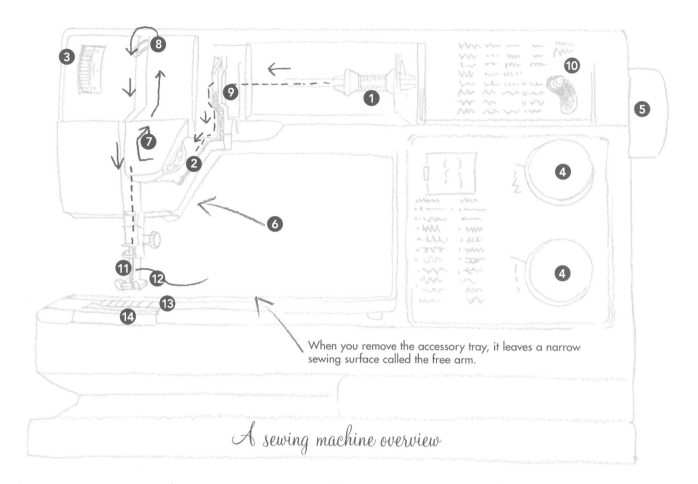

When you remove the accessory tray, it leaves a narrow sewing surface called the free arm.

*A sewing machine overview*

1. The spool holds the thread.

2. This dial adjusts the thread tension; turn it in tiny increments.

3. Adjust the pressure of the presser foot with this dial.

4. These dials adjust stitch selection, including width and length.

5. The handwheel revolves when you sew, and you can turn it by hand for precision work.

6. The presser foot lever (hiding in the back) lifts the presser foot and engages the tension disks. Remember to put it in the down position when you sew! But lift the presser foot when you thread your machine.

7. The tension disks, tucked inside the machine, regulate the movement of the thread.

8. The take-up lever carries the thread while the machine is sewing, pulling the exact amount it needs for each stitch. If this lever isn't threaded properly, an unsightly gob of thread will appear on your fabric.

9. The thread guides move the thread through the machine in an orderly fashion.

10. The bobbin winder winds the thread on the bobbin, of course.

11. The needle pierces the fabric and creates a stitch when it's looped together with the thread from the bobbin. Use the right size needle for your fabric, and use a new needle for each project.

12. The presser foot keeps the fabric snug against the feed dogs, the little serrated thingies that move the fabric as you sew.

13. The needle plate is the metal surface through which the needle grabs the bobbin thread. It has handy guidelines for seam allowances.

14. The bobbin is wound with thread and lives inside the machine. The looping of the thread from the spool with the thread from the bobbin forms the basic lockstitch.

between machines that might confuse you. For instance, the thread on my machine disappears inside for part of its journey—yours might not. My bobbin winds on the front of the machine—yours might be on top. I have a pressure foot dial, but you might have a lever. Despite that rambling disclaimer, I'd like to give you some general information about sewing machines. Let's give it a whirl.

See the illustration on the opposite page: a typical machine has a spool (or spools) for the thread; controls for stitch width, stitch length, thread tension, and presser foot pressure (say that three times fast); a handwheel; a take-up lever; tension disks; a presser foot lever; thread guides; a bobbin winder; a needle; a presser foot; feed dogs; a needle plate; and a bobbin. All of these things furiously work together to create the little lockstitch that makes a perfect pillow. Most modern machines have a detachable accessory tray that's part of the sewing surface; when it's removed, a narrow sewing surface called a *free arm* remains. The free arm lets you stitch inside pieces that are narrow, such as the end of a bolster.

In case you could have possibly forgotten (!), your sewing machine manual is the best source of information for your particular model. It will have detailed information about threading the machine; winding the bobbin; adjusting stitch width and length; and selecting any specialty stitches. Read through the manual thoroughly before you begin to make your pillow and practice stitching to familiarize yourself with the operation of your machine. It will be fun!

## Use the right needle

There's no great mystery to choosing the proper needle for your pillow. The three major types are sharps, for use on finely woven fabrics; ballpoints, for knits; and universal points, for all-purpose sewing on both knits and woven fabrics. Needles come in different sizes, with the smaller numbers for use on lightweight fabrics and the larger numbers for heavyweight material. They are marked in both European (60, 70, etc.) and American (10, 12, and so on) sizes; which number comes first depends on the manufacturer. A universal point in the medium range (80/12, for instance) will suit most of the fabric used in this book.

## Use the right presser foot

The presser foot is the gismo that keeps the fabric secure against the feed dogs; the feed dogs are the gismos that move the fabric along as you sew. There are lots of specialized presser feet designed to perform specific tasks, but we keep it simple in this book by using only two: a general presser foot that allows both straight and zigzag stitching, and the zipper foot, which lets you stitch close to the zipper when you're installing it. There's also a specialized zipper foot (all right, I guess that makes three kinds of presser feet) for putting in an invisible zipper, if you choose to use one of those. That handy manual of yours will instruct you on changing the presser feet.

# Got Sewing Machine?

*If you already have a sewing machine, you're ready to make a pillow. But, please hear this: The machine is really, really important, because if it doesn't operate properly, you won't be able to sew successfully. And you won't make any fabulous pillows.*

1 You don't have to spend a ton of money to get a perfectly good entry-level sewing machine. But you really should go to a dealer and test-drive before you buy. Sew over different thicknesses of fabric, thread it yourself, wind the bobbin, check out the stitch selection, make a buttonhole—dealers expect and welcome this level of scrutiny from their customers. Many dealers offer an introductory class after you've purchased a machine.

2 If you buy a used machine, insist on that test-drive, too. Stitching can look dreadfully wonky when there's actually not much wrong (maybe just a tension adjustment on the bobbin), but then again, maybe that poor machine has been abused. Have a reputable dealer inspect it before you plunk down your hard-earned cash. Make sure that you have a complete operating manual, too.

3 If you borrow a machine, please don't make the mistake of hauling a dusty machine out of someone's attic and thinking it will sew beautifully. Maybe it will, but probably it won't; sewing machines need to be tuned up regularly, just like cars. They work awfully hard, and they accumulate lots of dust from fabric and thread. (This dust migrates into the screwiest places, too.) Get a proper introduction from the machine's owner (do a lot of the same things I suggest when you're shopping for a machine) and have the owner point out its important features. Don't forget to borrow that manual, also. (As if!)

# Gather the
## Tools and Supplies

In addition to the sewing machine, you'll need to gather up a few other tools and materials before you begin your first pillow. All of these items are readily available at any fabric shop.

*For quick and easy cutting, use a rotary cutter, a cutting mat, and a clear ruler.*

**SCISSORS.** If you invest in only one quality item for making pillows, I suggest a good pair of 7- or 8-inch dressmaker's bent-handled shears. The design of bent-handled shears allows the fabric to remain flat, so it doesn't shift while you're cutting. A pair of sewing scissors, say 4 to 5 inches long, is perfect for other cutting tasks, such as trimming seams. Buy the best pair of scissors you can afford, because you'll be friends forever. I still use my grandmother's sewing scissors, which are at least 30 (if not 40) years old.

Though you should use dressmaker's shears to cut out your pillow, a pair of pinking shears is handy to finish seams. And they're cute, too.

**ROTARY CUTTER.** When you're cutting simple shapes, as you'll be doing when you make pillows, the rotary cutter is fast, efficient, and fun!

**SEAM RIPPER.** Change is inevitable, and so are mistakes.

17

Use a seam ripper to remove stitches that displease you.

**MEASURING TOOLS.** If the only measuring tool you had were a tape measure, you could certainly make a pillow. But a couple of other things are particularly useful, too. We can thank quilters for their cutting mats and clear rulers. Used in concert with a rotary cutter, these three tools make measuring and cutting a breeze. (They're are also very helpful when straightening fabric, which we'll talk about on pages 22 and 23.) A sewing gauge is a nifty little tool that has a slider for marking lengths, and you may it helpful when placing trim and buttonholes, for instance.

**PINS AND NEEDLES.** Basic dressmaker's pins will be fine for your early projects. Later on, you may want to add thin silk pins or long quilter's pins (with perky colorful heads) to your stash of sewing supplies. Quilter's pins can be quite useful when you're working with several layers of fabric, as you might do if you were making a box-edge pillow with piping, for instance.

You'll do very simple hand sewing for some the projects in this book. An assortment of sharps (all-purpose sewing needles) is fine.

**PINCUSHION.** Store all of your pins and needles in a pincushion. You can get the ubiquitous tomato or the groovy felt orb, or perhaps try a magnetic pincushion. Lately I've come to favor the magnetic variety because they can grab the pins that have misbehaved and escaped to the floor.

**THREAD.** All-purpose thread, which is cotton-wrapped polyester, is fine for any of the pillows in this book. As your adventure in sewing continues, you may eventually want to use all-cotton thread (great for woven, natural fiber fabrics) or perhaps all-polyester thread (good for fiber blends and knits). When you're choosing a thread color for your pillow, either match it to the fabric or choose a shade that's slightly darker.

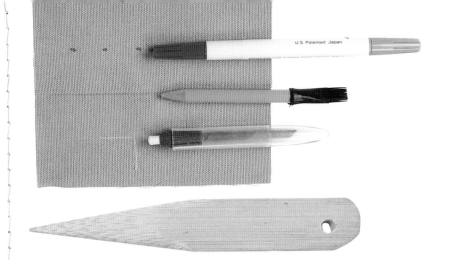

**POINT TURNER.** The point turner helps you push out sharp, crisp corners. If you want to.

**MARKING TOOLS.** Unlike garment sewing, where you have to mark lots of darts and circles and so on, you'll only need to make a few markings on your pillows. Occasionally, you'll need to mark a zipper opening or a buttonhole or something or other. There are a couple of different ways you can accomplish this: with tailor's chalk or a chalk pencil, or with a water-soluble or air-soluble (i.e., disappearing) fabric pen. You should always test your markers on a scrap of your fabric.

**MISCELLANEOUS NOTIONS.** In case you're interested, (and I'm sure you are), notions include all the other things you need to sew besides the fabric. We've already talked about the most important things you'll need, but here's a quick word about a few other items.

Several of our pillows have zippers, and a few have buttons (some functional, some not). We used *interfacing* in a project; interfacing is special fabric that's used to stabilize parts of your pillow. The interfacing used in this book is fusible, which means that it bonds to the fabric with heat and pressure.

**DECORATIVE ELEMENTS.** Ribbon, lace, buttons, beads, appliqués—we've got it all. Read all about decorative techniques on page 45.

**IRON.** An iron is a very important tool in all types of sewing, but its use can be limited when you make a pillow. When you iron a skirt, for instance, you can slide the skirt on the ironing board to press the seams.

Sometimes you can't do that with a pillow, especially after all the sides have been sewn. See the photo above for a demonstration of pressing the seams in a pillow.

Note that we're not talking about *ironing*, which is sliding your iron across the fabric. We're talking about *pressing*. Pressing is moving the iron across the fabric in increments by pressing it up and down. If you can, press open each seam before it's overlapped by another seam. If you can't, you can *finger press* the seams open. It's exactly as it sounds, which is pressing the seams open with pressure from your fingers.

Guess what? We're ready to start sewing. Grab a cup of java.

# Learn to Sew!

I kid you not—a pillow is the most painless introduction to sewing imaginable. We're going cut the fabric; mark the pieces, if we need to; stitch up the pillow; and insert the pillow form. Sewing is really a lot like the process of cooking: you choose a recipe (the pillow style); buy the ingredients (the fabric and notions); do the washing and chopping (preparing and cutting out the fabric); and then add the ingredients to one another according to the recipe (sew by following the project instructions). See—a piece of cake. Or, if you'd rather—easy as pie.

*Let's get started by readying our fabric.*

## Prepare the fabric

You have to know a little more about fabric to understand the importance of the proper layout and subsequent cutting of your pillow, so bear with me a moment. When we discussed fabric earlier, we talked about prewashing. Now, prewashing actually means *shrinking,* as many washable fabrics will do just that when laundered. Generally, the looser the weave, the more shrinkage is likely to occur. Washing also removes sizing or finishes that may affect the quality of your stitches. Check the label on the bolt of cloth for the laundering recommendations, and launder the fabric the same way you plan to launder the pillow. Please don't neglect this very important step,

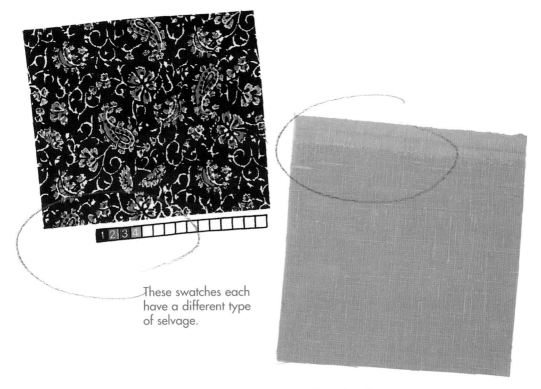

These swatches each have a different type of selvage.

because you'll be totally bummed to wash your pillow for the first time and then find that it's way too small for its pillow form! After you've laundered your fabric, press it to remove any wrinkles. (Remember: press, not iron.)

## Align the grain

Your fabric must be correctly aligned before you cut out the pillow pieces, and here's why. (We'll get to the how in just a few minutes.) Woven fabric is made of lengthwise and crosswise threads. In a perfect world, the crosswise threads are perpendicular to the lengthwise threads. The direction of these threads is called the *grain*. Let's look at figure 3 while we're talking.

Your pillow pieces must follow the proper direction of the grain, or the pieces won't fit together as they should. Most garment pieces follow the lengthwise (or straight) grain, because the lengthwise threads are designed to be stronger to withstand the tension of the weaving process. The finished border on the length of the fabric is the *selvage*. This border differs in appearance from fabric to fabric. You should also know about *bias*; the bias flows along the diagonal between the lengthwise and

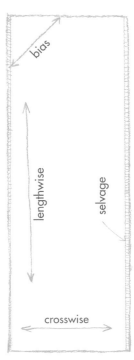

FIGURE 3

21

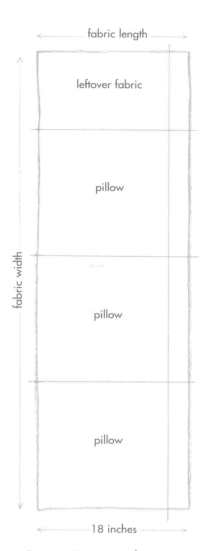

fabric length

leftover fabric

pillow

pillow

pillow

fabric width

18 inches

FIGURE 4. You can get three 15 x 15-inch pillow tops on ¹/₂ yard of 54-inch fabric by cutting them out across the width.

crosswise threads. This is the direction in which woven fabric has the most stretch. We'll take advantage of this property when we learn how to make our own piping later on in this chapter.

You may want to cut out your pillow pieces across the width to conserve fabric. This is perfectly fine, as you'll still have the benefit of the strong lengthwise threads. See figure 4 for an explanation of what I mean; it saves you from having to purchase extra yardage that you don't need.

To check the grain, first fold the fabric and align the selvages. Smooth out the fabric so it's flat. If you can't get the wrinkles out and the fabric won't lie flat, you may need to straighten the crosswise edges and try again. Why? Sometimes the length of the fabric wasn't perfectly cut along a crosswise thread. If you're starting to get that creepy home ec feeling, chill: this is easier than it sounds, I promise. To find a crosswise thread on a woven fabric, clip into the selvage and pull out a crosswise thread across the entire width of the fabric. Then, trim the edge even along this visible line, as you see so easily done in the illustration below. Fold the fabric again, aligning the crosswise ends and the selvages; the ends and the selvages should be perpendicular to one another.

If your fabric seems too thick to pull out a thread (and some decorator fabrics may be), try something else. Use the cutting mat and clear ruler to straighten the crosswise edges as shown on the next page, or use a carpenter's square (one of those shiny L-shaped rulers your dad had in his workshop) to do the same thing.

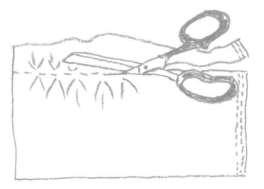

*Straightening the fabric ends*

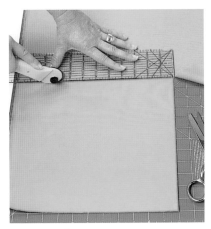

Cutting out the pieces

## Cut out the pillow pieces

Let's pretend we're still working on those 14 x 14-inch knife-edge pillows we talked about on page 12. (That poor sofa still needs some sprucing up.) How shall we cut them out? We could either fold the fabric, to cut the front and back at the same time, or we could cut the pieces individually (if we were using a different fabric on the front and back, for instance).

Remember we said that the standard pillow is cut 1 inch larger in each direction than the size of the pillow form. When you use a 1/2-inch seam allowance, you end up with a pillow that's exactly the same size as the pillow form, for a nice snug fit. You see how easy it is to transfer this formula to any size pillow form—if the form is 14 x 18 inches, cut the pieces to 15 x 19 inches. (Here's a secret; if you want a nice plump pillow, use slightly larger seam allowances, say 5/8 inch, instead of 1/2 inch. It's not often we *want* things to be plump, is it?)

After straightening the edges, either fold the fabric and align the edges, or lay it flat. Use the cutting mat, rotary cutter, and clear ruler to cut the pieces to the correct size. If you don't have these tools, use a ruler or tape measure to mark the pieces and cut them out with scissors. If you need to make any markings, do so now, on the wrong side of the fabric.

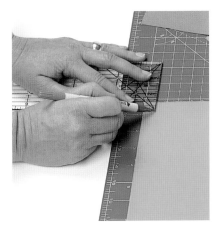

Marking the pillow front

# Start to sew

Okay, girlfriends, we're ready to sew. I hope you're as excited as I am! We've chosen a pillow style, purchased the fabric and notions, and cut out and marked the pieces. Read through the next section and promise me you'll sit down at the sewing machine and practice stitching before you get started. Remember to familiarize yourself with your sewing machine and its controls (did I already tell you this?), and set up your workspace so all your tools and materials are handy.

In the following section, we'll talk about the basic techniques that we've used in our pillow projects. Don't try to remember everything at once, but read it through so you have a general understanding of the process. Later, in the Make a Pillow! section, you'll see how the techniques work in context when you make your own pillow. We've presented them here with

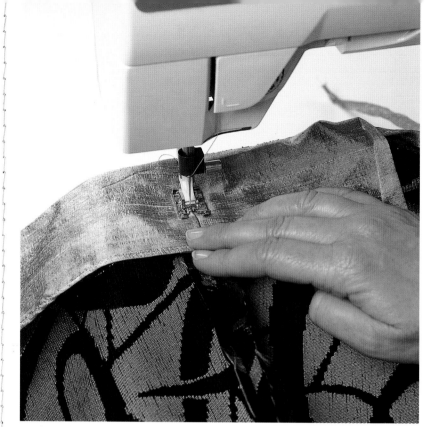

Stitching the facing of the Tie-End Pillow (page 55)

contrasting stitching so you can easily see what happens during each step. Furthermore, we've used fabric that's similar to what we used for many of our pillows (cotton), so you can see real-world examples of how these fabrics behave when they're sewn. This isn't computer-enhanced sewing we're doing here.

And you may notice real-world sewing in the Make a Pillow! section, too—fabrics fray when they're handled and some techniques (like gathering) put more stress on the material, so you'll probably see a thread or two. You'll see them on your own pillows as well. Since you're learning, you shouldn't be overly stressed out about what the inside of your pillow looks like, but do tidy it up when you're done, trimming all the loose threads. This isn't work now—it's *fun* and you're just beginning. So plug in the machine, turn on the lights, and let's sew. If you need a refresher course when you're making your pillow, you can always flip back to these illustrated techniques.

## Stitch a seam

To avoid boggling your mind, we've kept the sewing fairly simple in *Fun & Fabulous Pillows,* using only basic techniques. There are three stitches: the straight stitch, the basting stitch, and the zigzag. The straight stitch is the foundation of your pillow; you can also do the straight stitch in reverse to anchor the beginning of your seams or to provide reinforcement at certain points, such as a zipper opening. (Consult our friend The Manual for reverse stitching.) The basting stitch is simply a straight stitch set to a longer length. Use basting stitches to temporarily hold layers together or to gather fabric. Zigzag stitches are used to finish the raw edges of seams, or for just plain fun.

When you're practicing, use a contrasting thread so you can easily see your stitches. Also, use two pieces of fabric for the best results; sewing machines

*Our 3 helpful stitches*

Basting stitch

Zigzag stitch

Straight stitch

are designed to join two layers of fabric, so the top and bobbin stitches meet in the middle. Refer to You Know What for the proper way to thread your machine, wind the bobbin, and accurately set the stitch length. A setting of 10–12 stitches per inch is average for the type of sewing we're doing.

To sew a seam, align the fabric edges and pin them together with the pins perpendicular, the heads near the edge. Line up the fabric to the 1/2-inch guideline on your sewing machine's needle plate, because 1/2-inch seam allowances are standard in home décor sewing. Place the

Gently hold the threads when you begin stitching.

fabric underneath the needle just a tiny bit (oh, ¼ inch) from the end of the fabric. Lower the presser foot (do remember to do this because gnarly things happen if you forget). Hold the bobbin and top threads while you backstitch a couple of stitches to the end of the seam. Let go of the threads and stitch forward, pausing to remove the pins as you go. Don't, don't, *don't be* tempted to stitch over the pins—you can break a needle, or worse, ruin your machine's timing by hitting a pin. Or even worse, have shards of metal flying around you and your pillow.

Guide the fabric lightly with your hands, keeping it straight against the guideline on your

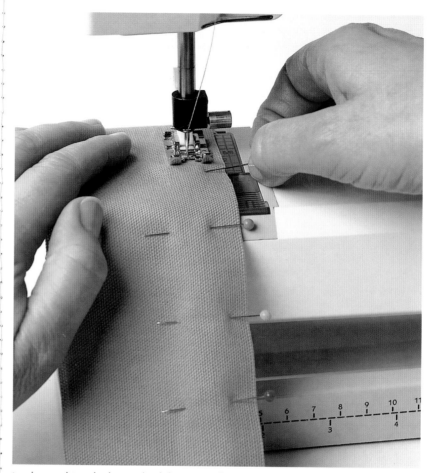

Let the machine do the work while you guide the fabric. Remove the pins before you reach them.

needle plate. Watch the guideline and not the needle—it can be hypnotizing. (You may think I'm kidding, but I'm not!) Let the machine do the work of pulling the fabric along (that's what those busy little feed dogs do). When you reach the end of the seam, backstitch for a few stitches to secure.

*Congratulations—you've just stitched your first seam. Relax and have some tea.*

## Balance the tension

After your tea (and maybe a snack, too), take a moment to admire your first seam. Look at both sides of the fabric; the stitches should be nearly identical on each side, being locked between the two pieces of fabric. If they don't look identical, you may need to adjust the thread tension on your machine. Each thread (top and bobbin) has its own tension. You'll probably need to make adjustments to the tension according to the type of fabric you're using to make your pillow. Every time you sew with a new fabric, you should check the tension first.

The examples at the right show correct tension; top tension that's too tight; and top tension that's too loose. When the top tension is too tight, it yanks the poor bobbin thread up to the right side of the fabric; the opposite happens when the top tension is too loose. Following the instructions in (guess what?) your manual, make small adjustments at a time and do test seams until you're happy with the tension setting.

To check thread tension, use different colors of the same type of thread—one color (pink) on top, the other (white) in the bobbin.

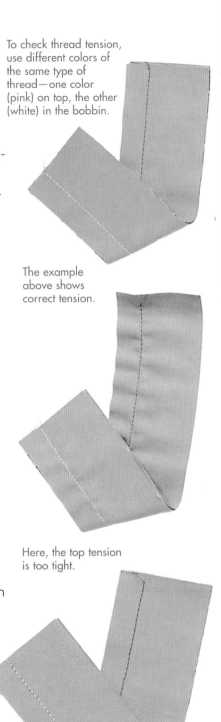

The example above shows correct tension.

Here, the top tension is too tight.

This example shows top tension that's too loose.

## Pivot

When you're sewing, you occasionally have to change direction—just like driving. Since we're making lots of square things in this book, you'll certainly have to pivot. When you need to do an about-face, you do so like this: Stop with the needle in the fabric. Raise your presser foot and turn the fabric. Lower your presser foot and have at it!

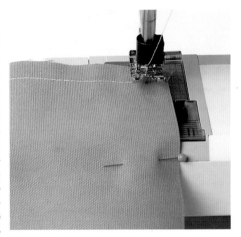

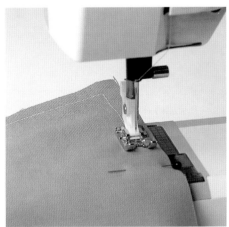

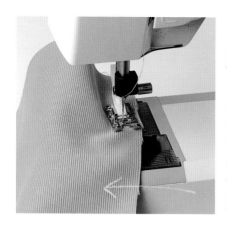

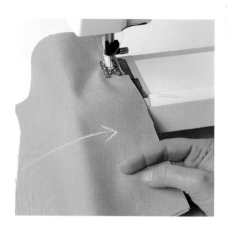

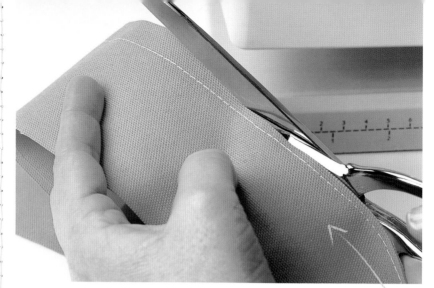

## Trim seams and clip curves

At certain points along the way you may need to trim a seam, especially if you're using heavy fabric. Our project instructions will tell you when to do this. Generally, you trim a seam to reduce bulk in the finished pillow. Simply use your shears to trim away the seam allowance to about ¼ inch.

Curved seams demand a little extra attention. In this book, you can make curved corners for your pillows, instead of square ones. If you do, you'll need to notch the curves every inch or so to allow the seams to lie flat inside the pillow. Cut notches in the seam allowance to eliminate fullness, using just the tips of the scissors, or use your pinking shears for quickie notching.

## Guide the fabric

Sometimes, you don't need a complete change of direction, just some friendly guidance. Use a gentle pull of the fabric to keep the fabric aligned on your needle plate.

## Reinforce and clip the corners

I've always found that my corners turn easier, and look better, if I reinforce them with an extra line of stitching and then clip the corners. And since it's my book, I'm telling you to do this, too.

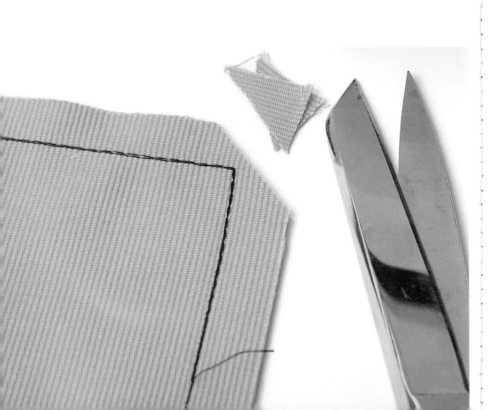

# Finish the seams

Conventional sewing wisdom says that all seams should be finished in some manner, to prevent raveling and increase the longevity of your project. Sounds like good advice to me. Several of the seam finishes used in garment sewing don't work so well on a pillow, and some others require specialized presser feet. Let's focus on a few simple methods you can use if the spirit moves you.

**ZIGZAG.** If you want to finish the seams before you sew, sew a line of zigzag stitching into the seam allowance, as close to the cut edge as you can. This is a good choice for fabrics that tend to ravel easily. After stitching the seam, press it open. If you're using a lightweight fabric, you might find that it's a little tricky to stitch into the single thickness without the fabric puckering, so use one of the methods that follow instead.

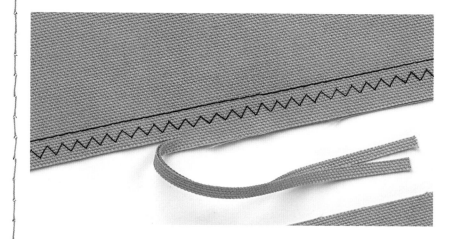

**DOUBLE-STITCHED.** The double-stitched seam is suitable for light-weight fabrics. After the seam has been sewn, stitch a parallel line of stitching in the seam allowance, then trim away close to the second line of stitching. Press to one side. (You could do a second line of stitching in a frisky little zigzag, too.)

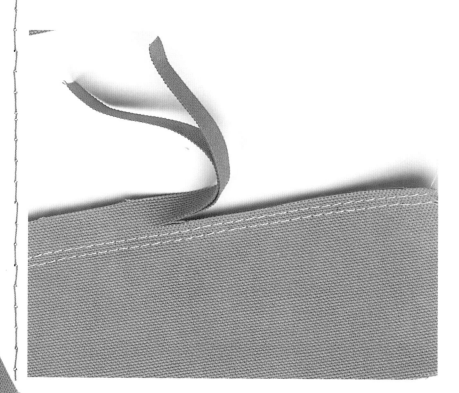

**PINKED.** This is a good choice for tightly woven fabrics. After stitching the seam, trim with pinking shears. Press open to finish.

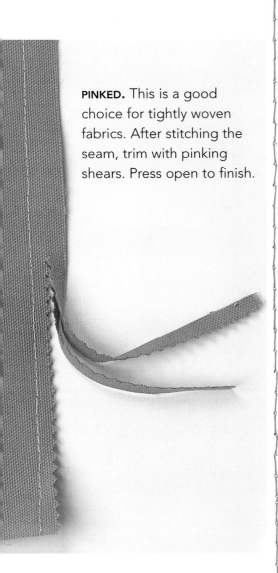

## Right sides together

You'll almost always sew the pieces of your pillow with the right sides together (facing each other). This is the most basic fact you need to remember about sewing in general. If your fabric doesn't have easily recognizable right and wrong sides, be sure to mark each piece so you can quickly determine which is which.

## Make a narrow hem

Several of the pillows in this book have edges that are finished with narrow hems. It's just like it sounds: a skinny little hem that's stitched in place on the machine. Typically they're made like this: Stitch ½ inch or so from the raw edge and press up along this line of stitching. Tuck under the raw edge to meet the stitching, forming a nice fold. Press and stitch in place along the fold.

## Add a closure

You're probably smart enough to figure out that you can use any closure you want as long as you've planned the construction of your pillow accordingly. I touched on this before, but deciding whether your pillow will have a removable form will impact the kind of closure you use. For example, you can stitch up all four sides, with no plans to ever remove the insides or launder the pillow, and tra la la, you're done. Or, you could add a sham closing, or a zipper, so you can take out the pillow form with ease. If you want to put a zipper in, though, you've got to do it before you stitch all the other seams in place, so there's where the planning comes in.

One other consideration is whether you want your pillow to be reversible—whether the back is going to be as beautiful as the front, in other words. For example, you could use different fabrics on the front and the back and flip your pillow over for an occasional change of pace.

Here are various ways to close your pillow: remember that you should decide how you want to close the pillow *before* you cut out the pieces. You have lots of options. There are a few specialty closures that we use in the Make a Pillow! section, too, that you may find amusing.

*Here's the front and the back of the Collage Pillow (page 96). Can you find the closure?*

*Hint: it's invisible.*

32

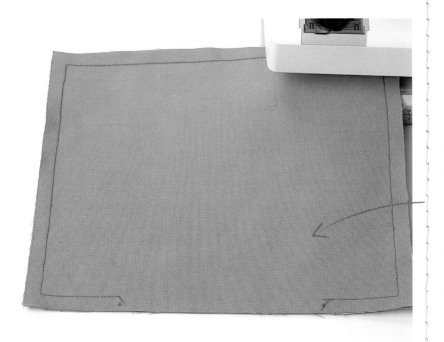

**STITCH IT CLOSED.** This is the quickest and easiest way to make a pillow. Stitch around the sides of the pillow, leaving an opening on one side. Turn the pillow right side out (remember you've stitched it with the right sides facing), and press under the seam allowances on the opening. Pin it closed; stitch together by machine or by hand. (We'll talk more about hand stitches on page 44.) If you stitch it by machine, you form a neat little flange around the edge of the pillow. Here's a tip: if you stuff your pillow with a polyester-filled form, you'll probably find it easier to slipstitch the opening by hand. This method is great for a reversible pillow.

Actually, if you don't mind a little unsewing (i.e., ripping out your stitches), you could take the form out if your pillow ever needs an unexpected cleaning.

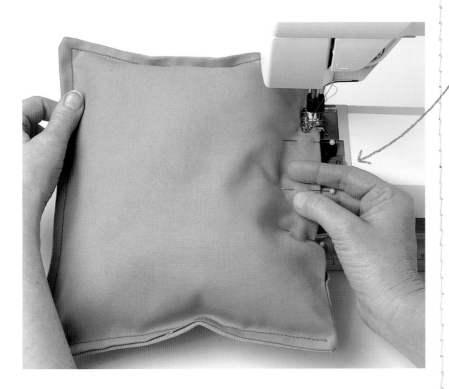

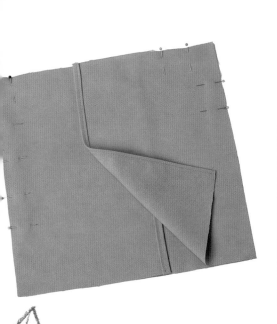

**OVERLAP IT CLOSED**. You know what a sham is, don't you? Well, shams have an overlap closure in the back, so you can stuff the pillow form inside. You can make this same closure on your pillows, too. To use this method, cut out the pillow back about 5 or 6 inches wider than the front. Now, cut that piece in half across the width and hem the edges. Pin one piece of the pillow back to the pillow front, right sides together. Overlap the other back piece, and pin and stitch all the sides. Turn right side out through the overlap. Obviously, this method yields only one beautiful side—the front.

**BUTTON IT CLOSED**. You can place a row of buttons (and corresponding buttonholes, of course) along any side of your pillow. I'm going to cop out and ask you to refer to your sewing machine manual to learn about making buttonholes, because the procedure is a little different from machine to machine. Just know that this is yet another way to make your cover easily removable, but it also creates a distinctive front and back, because the buttons will only show on the front. What's more, you can make custom covered buttons with kits you'll find at any fabric store.

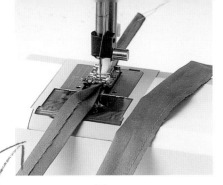

**TIE IT CLOSED.** There are a couple of ways you can make ties for your pillows. The easiest tie is on the left, above: Cut a piece of fabric to the length you want the tie. Fold it in half lengthwise and press; turn each raw edge into the center and press again. Stitch in place.

Making a tube, shown on the right above, is slightly more involved, but not much. Stitch a length of fabric together with the right sides facing and—presto!—turn it inside out. There are several gadgets you can buy to turn tubes, or you can just attach a safety pin to one end and thread the pin back through the tube, pulling it right side out.

You can make reversible pillows with tie closures.

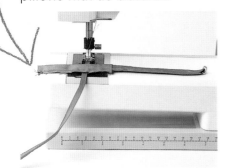

**ZIP IT CLOSED.** They don't call 'em zippers for nothing, you know! Nothing's faster than unzipping a zipper to remove the pillow form. All the zippers we installed in this book were placed in the bottom seam, between the front and the back, so you can make reversible pillows with this technique, too. One fabulous thing about nylon-coil zippers is that you can trim them to any length you want. (You'll see what I mean in a minute.)

CENTERED ZIPPER. There are several ways to put in a zipper, so how about we pick an easy one? The basic centered zipper is about as simple as it gets. You install a zipper in a seam that's partially sewn, centering the zipper in the middle of the seam. Here's how to start. After pinning together the bottom edge of the front and back of the pillow, center the zipper along this edge and mark the location of the zipper stops. (You'll see the zipper stops at the top and bottom of the zipper teeth.) You'll stitch to these marks on each end. Now…

1 After stitching the seam to the appropriate spot at each end, backstitch for a few stitches to anchor. Baste the rest of the seam between the marks and press it open. This is where the zipper goes.

Photo 1

2 Place the zipper facedown on the basted seam. Put the zipper foot on your machine. Pin the zipper in place and baste, stitching the same direction (i.e., bottom to top) on each side (photo 1). Contrasting thread makes it easy to see the basting stitches when you have to remove them later on.

35

3 Reduce the stitch length to a normal setting. Begin at the seam below the zipper stop, stitch about ¼ inch, pivot, and stitch up the side. If you'd like a nice clean line to follow, use piece of quilter's tape to mark the stitching line, as we did here. Repeat on the other side (photo 2), pivoting at the top and stitching across to the other line of stitching.

4 Remove the basting stitches along the sides of the zipper (photo 3). Finally, rip the basting stitches in the seam to reveal your zipper. It's finished (photo 4). Isn't it beautiful?

TRIM A ZIPPER. Sometimes you may have an odd-sized opening in your pillow. If so, you can install a long zipper into the opening and trim away the excess afterward. If you simply cut off the excess zipper, the zipper pull might come off if you unzipped it with too much gusto. So you have to make a new zipper stop by whipstitching back and forth over the teeth, just above the spot where you've trimmed the zipper. But in the zipper applications we've used in this book, it's pretty hard to unzip the zipper far enough to dislodge the

Photo 2

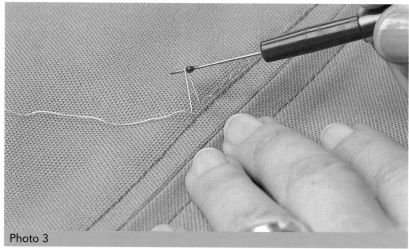
Photo 3

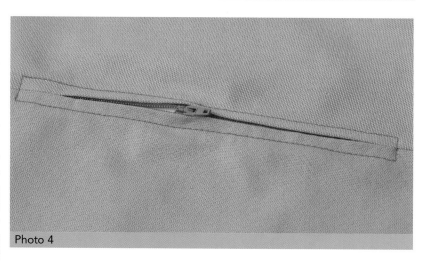
Photo 4

pull, because the zippers are contained within a seam that won't allow such foolishness. But, just to be on the safe side, go ahead and whipstitch across the coils where you want your new (and improved!) zipper stop to be before you install the zipper. Trim away the extra zipper after you've sewn it in place.

INVISIBLE ZIPPER. And it is just about invisible, too. This zipper has teeth that curl to the underside when it's zipped up. To install this zipper most successfully, you'll need a specialized zipper foot. Sewing machine manufacturers and zipper manufacturers make these feet, so you can buy one that specifically matches your machine *or* the zipper. Although I'm going to give you general instructions below, you should be sure to read the instructions that come with your invisible zipper foot. They could vary slightly from what I've told you here.

Invisible zippers aren't available in the range of lengths that regular zippers are, but guess what? You can trim a nylon-coil invisible zipper to the length you need, too. It's very easy—just trim off the bottom of the zipper after it's sewn in place. In fact, some manufacturers advise you to *always* buy a zipper that's several inches longer than the zipper opening. Because of the installation of the invisible zipper, the pull is even less likely to come off, as long as you remember to leave that extra inch or two of zipper. Here we go…

1 Unlike a centered zipper, the invisible zipper is installed *before* any part of the seam is sewn. And very unlike a centered zipper, the right sides of the zipper tape should face the right sides of the fabric, with the zipper teeth at the seamline. Begin by unzipping the zipper and pressing the coils flat with an iron set to the synthetic setting. Place the coils under the groove in the zipper foot. Using the invisible zipper foot, stitch one side of the zipper tape from top to bottom, stitching as close to the zipper stop as you can. Backstitch at each end to secure. (If you're shortening a zipper, you'll need to mark the spot to which you want to stitch, as we did in photo 5.)

Photo 5

2 To stitch the other side, again place the right side of the zipper tape to the right side of the fabric. (Not right as in right or left, but right as in right vs. wrong.) Note how the zipper looks at this point (photo 6).

Photo 6

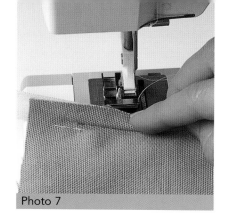

Photo 7

3 After stitching both sides of the zipper, place the pillow front and back together, right sides facing, and use the regular zipper foot to finish the seam, starting above the last few stitches of the zipper installation. In photo 7, you see that the zipper was installed with blue thread, and the seam has been sewn with white thread. Inevitably, there will be a tiny gap between the zipper and the seam, but it will be barely noticeable if you use your regular zipper foot to stitch the seam.

4 See how invisible it is! Only the zipper pulls shows on the right side of the fabric (photo 8).

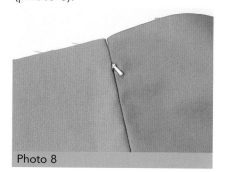

Photo 8

QUICK ZIPPER. Once you get the hang of sewing, you may get adept enough to skip many of the steps in the centered zipper. So, here's something to look forward to.

1 Begin this quickie zipper just like a centered zipper, by pinning the front and back of the pillow together and centering the zipper on the fabric. Mark the zipper stops. You'll stitch to these marks on each end and backstitch a few stitches to anchor. Now, simply press open the seam and you'll see a gap where the zipper will go (photo 9).

Photo 9

2 Center the zipper in the opening and sew it in place, stitching from top to bottom on each side (photo 10). No pins or basting required!

Photo 10

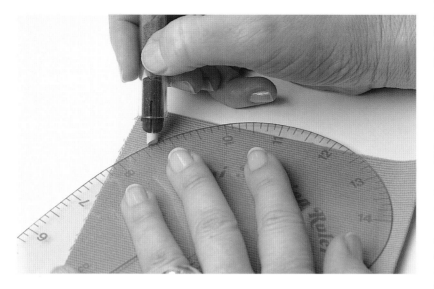

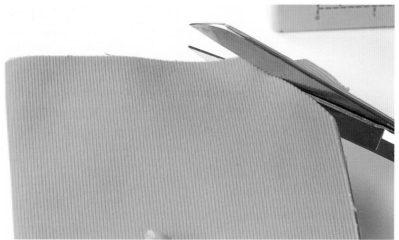

## Square corners? Round corners?

Another little decision you have to make about your pillow is whether it will have square corners or round corners. It's your call. Some people don't like the "dog-eared" look of pillows with square corners; if you're one of those people, here's what you do.

Fold your pillow front in half, and in half again, this time from the opposite direction. Find the edge with no folds and use a dressmaker's curve, or any kind of curved object, and trace a curved line. Trim the corner along the line you just drew. Use this piece as a template and cut out the pillow back.

## Add a facing

A facing is a piece of fabric that finishes an edge. We've used facings on our pillows that have tie closures, and you'll learn how to add one in the projects section. But it's simple: it's your basic right-sides-together, stitch-and-turn sort of thing.

## Add piping

Ah, piping. It's a pretty conventional technique, but it can certainly add a lot of *joie de vivre* to a project. Of course, you can purchase piping, but we're going to learn to make it ourselves. We're all about DIY in this book, boys and girls.

Piping is a wonderful accent for your pillows, and it's a great way to customize your projects. What you need to do first is cut some bias strips. (Remember, the bias is the stretchy part of a piece of fabric—because the piping will

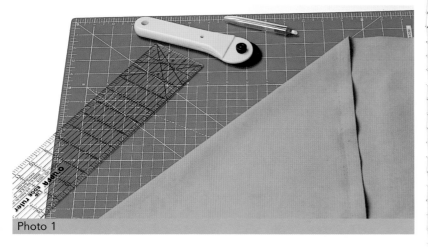
Photo 1

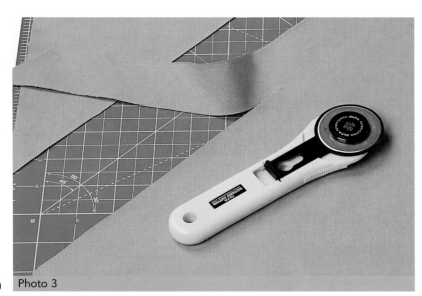
Photo 2

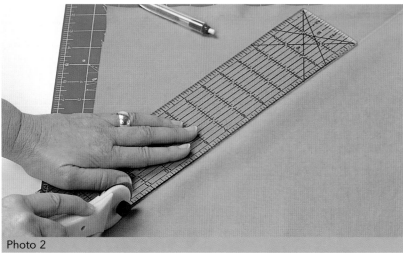

run around your pillow, it needs the stretch.) Then, you'll wrap the bias strips around a strip of cording.

First, fold the fabric to find the bias. You can fold the selvage all the way up to the cut edge, or cheat and use the marked lines on your cutting mat (photo 1). I'm a cheater, because I save a little fabric this way. Mark the fold and cut along the line (photo 2), and then cut strips with this line as a guide (photo 3). The magical clear ruler makes this a snap.

Cut the bias strips wide enough to wrap around the cording and leave a ¹/₂-inch seam allowance. (You can just wrap the fabric around the cording and measure to figure this out.) You'll have to piece the strips together to reach your desired length, so stitch them together with the right sides facing. Note that the pieces are slightly offset and should form a right angle (photo 4).

Photo 4

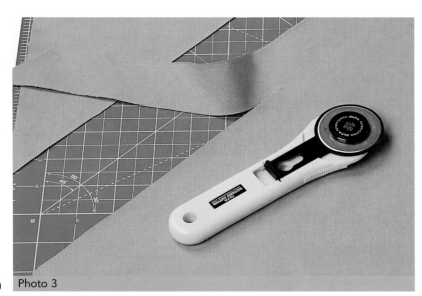
Photo 3

Now, let's add the cording. Wrap the bias strip around the cording, centering it on the wrong side of the strip. Use your zipper foot to stitch close to the cording; it's very easy to do this without pinning (photo 5).

You'll add your snazzy piping to the pillow by inserting it between the front and back of the pillow. Place the piping along the cut edge of the pillow front and baste it in place with the zipper foot, starting at least 1 inch from the end of the strip. Baste all the way around, clipping at the corners (photo 6). You can pin the piping in place if you need to. When you're about 2 inches from the end, stop with the needle in the fabric. Rip out enough stitches in the piping to uncover the cording (photo 7), and trim the cording so the two ends are flush. Fold under one end of the fabric and cover the other end of the strip. Complete the line of stitching (photo 8).

We're not opposed to using store-bought trim, either. Add purchased trim as in photo 9, overlapping the ends into the seam allowance.

There's another nifty way of joining together strips that have no cording inside (flat piping, so to speak. Well, actually, it's called a flange). See this method on page 70, in the projects section.

Photo 5

Photo 6

Photo 7

Photo 8

Photo 9

## Add a boxing strip

When you want a firm pillow, add a boxing strip. This strip of fabric encases the perimeter of a pillow, whether square or round. The boxing strip creates the tailored look of a box-edge pillow (remember this pillow is the same depth throughout). We've used foam inserts on all the box-edge pillows in this book.

You'll place a boxing strip between the front and back of the pillow. Typically, there's a zipper in the boxing strip to allow access for the pillow form. Although we've also added piping to all of our box-edge pillows, it's certainly not a requirement.

The boxing strip should be as wide as the depth of the pillow, plus 1 inch, and as long as the circumference of the pillow, plus 1 inch. Here's the skinny: if your pillow form is 24 x 24 inches square and 4 inches thick, you'll need a strip that measures 5 x 97 inches. You've probably figured out that you'll have to piece together two (or more) strips to reach the length you need, and you'll have to install the zipper in one of the strips. You'll need to add yet another inch in width to allow for the zipper. So, cut two pieces for

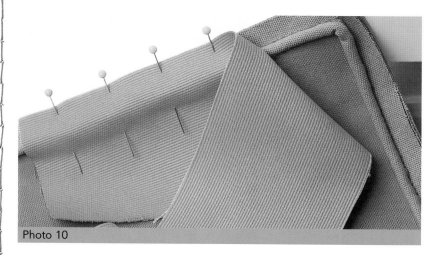

Photo 10

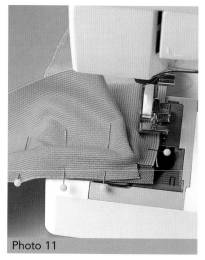

Photo 11

Photo 12

the boxing strip, one piece that's 6 x 49 inches and one piece that's 5 x 49 inches. Cut the 6-inch piece in half lengthwise and install the zipper in this piece.

Stitch the ends of the boxing strip together, right sides facing, to form a continuous strip. You may want to check the fit before you add it to the pillow.

Now, to the nitty-gritty. Pin the boxing strip to the pillow front, right sides facing (photo 10). When you get to the corners, clip the boxing strip and fold it as shown to eliminate any puckers at the corners (photo 11). Unzip the zipper and repeat on the pillow back; turn the pillow right side out through the zipper opening. Here's how your boxing strip will look (photo 12). Isn't it smart?

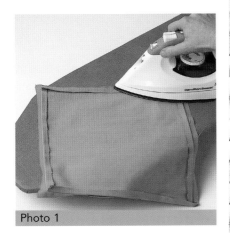

Photo 1

Photo 2

Photo 3

## Make a mock-box pillow

Not ready to tackle a box-edge pillow, but you like the look? Here's the quick-and-dirty version, the mock-box pillow. You cut out this pillow as you would a knife-edge pillow, and stitch up the sides the same way. But here's the difference.

Press the seams open (photo 1). At the corners, pull the seams together and align them. To check the alignment, place a pin horizontally above the fold and turn the pillow inside out. Adjust the join of the seams if necessary, and secure the alignment by sticking a pin through the seams; it should be smack dab in the center of each seam. Pin in place (photo 2).

Measure from the corner and mark a line that's half the depth of the pillow; in this case, a 3-inch pillow was marked 1 1/2 inches from the corner. Stitch across the marked line, backstitching at each end of the seam. Repeat for each corner. Turn inside out; here's how your perfectly matched corner will look (photo 3). Stuff with fiberfill or a square form.

## Custom pillow

If you're the adventurous type and want to make your pillows in some crazy size, you can easily make your own custom pillow forms. Use cotton *muslin* (or some other thin, inexpensive fabric) and cut it to the size and shape you want, remembering to add that extra inch to each dimension. Stitch the muslin together in 1/2-inch seams, leaving an opening on one side. Stuff to your desired plumpness with fiberfill, and stitch the opening. As you can see, your pillow form doesn't have to be astonishingly beautiful to be perfectly functional. You don't even have to use matching thread!

43

## Stitch by hand

You only need a few basic hand stitches to make the pillows in this book. Begin all hand stitching with a knot in your thread; make a simple loop in the end and pull the needle through. Sometimes a second knot is necessary to keep the thread from pulling through the fabric.

Finish a line of hand stitching in one of two ways. Make a series of backstitches (a small stitch made from left to right and repeated several times in place). You can also make a quick knot. Make a wee stitch on top of your last stitch on the wrong side of your fabric, forming a small loop. Pull the needle through the loop until a second loop forms. Pull the needle through the second loop tightly to form a knot.

The stitch you're likely to use most is the slipstitch, a fairly invisible little stitch. In this book, the slipstitch is used between two folded edges, closing up a seam.

Begin a slipstitch from the wrong side. Insert the needle into the fold of the fabric and pull the thread. Work from right to left as you pick up just a thread or two in one fold and then insert the needle into the fold opposite the first stitch. Repeat, making stitches every ¼ inch or so.

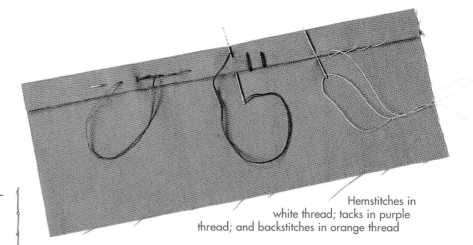

Hemstitches in white thread; tacks in purple thread; and backstitches in orange thread

There are several other hand stitches you may find useful. We just discussed the backstitch; the tack is simply a straight stitch used to join layers of fabric. You can repeat them in place, or make a series of straight stitches. Use a tack to sew on a button.

If you want to hem anything by hand, use the hemstitch. A hemstitch is begun with the needle inserted into the fold of the fabric. Work from right to left as you pick up just a thread or two in the fabric and then insert the needle into the edge of the fold above the first stitch; it should be pretty much perpendicular to the fold. Repeat, making stitches every ¼ inch or so.

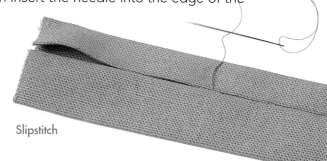

Slipstitch

## Fix a mistake

The best way to fix a mistake is to avoid it in the first place, but of course, we all make them, even the most experienced seamstresses (especially when our caffeine level is low). There's not much that can't be repaired by simply ripping out all the stitches and trying again. When you're using a seam ripper to remove stitches, be careful not to tear the fabric by ripping too enthusiastically. I know how much fun it can be. (Catch the sarcasm?)

If you're having a weak moment and feel unsure about something you've just stitched, chill a second and make sure it's correct before you do any trimming or clipping.

# Embellish Your Pillow

Photo 1

Sometimes a pillow needs a little TLC to make it extra special. The pillow front is a perfect little canvas to decorate. You'll add the bells, whistles, and flourishes before you actually begin to sew the pillow together. Here are a few ways that we've adorned our pillows with embellishments.

Add decorative trim to make your pillow more beautiful. In photo 1, we've merely stitched this luxurious trim onto the front of the pillow before it was constructed. You can use decorative stitching when you're sewing on trim, too (photo 2). Experiment with the placement and pin the pieces in place before you begin, if necessary.

Photo 2

We also used ribbon to make medallions that accented the motifs on our fabric. In photo 3, we whipped out our hand sewing needles and backstitched a length of vintage rayon trim to the pillow, after first folding and pressing it in half. A print fabric can be great inspiration for this type of embellishment.

A few stitches of embroidery can perk up any pillow. There are really cool flosses on the market now (rayon, silk, variegated, metallic, etc.) for

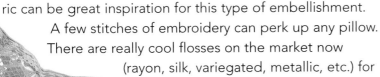

Photo 3

Photo 4

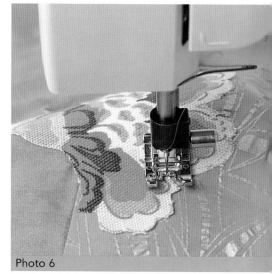
Photo 6

your decorating pleasure. We used embroidery to accent pieces of fabric (photo 4) and to create funky little motifs (photo 5). Embroidery doesn't have to be elaborate to make a statement, as you can easily see.

We had a lot of fun with appliqués in this book—we stitched 'em on, we fused 'em on, and we decorated 'em with embroidery. If you fuse them on, which is a very quick and easy way to add appliqués to your pillows, be sure that your fabric can withstand the heat of the fusing process. And of course,

you can fuse them and *then* stitch them, too, as the fusing holds them in place and makes the stitching a bit easier. The appliqué on the pillow in photo 6 was created this way. This pillow looks so great because the appliqué is set on a background of different fabrics, creating lots of visual interest.

Because we think you're so cool, we've included some additional techniques you can use to embellish your pillows on page 106. It's free with the purchase of *Fun & Fabulous Pillows!*

Photo 5

# Use This Book

All right, people, we've discussed just about everything you really need to know about making a pillow. We've looked at how-to photographs and illustrations. I'm just about ready to turn it over to you. Here are a few things to keep in mind before you start to sew.

**CHOOSE YOUR PROJECT.** We've got three basic pillow styles in this book—the knife-edge pillow, the box-edge pillow, and the bolster. The knife-edge pillow is the easiest, as you can just cut out two squares of fabric, stitch it up, and stuff. But remember about all the other variations we talked about—using different closures, adding piping, decorating your pillow—and think about what you want your pillows to look like. Our 15 projects include some interesting variations, so we invite you to peruse them all before you decide where to start.

Generally speaking, the pillows are presented in categories according to ease of construction, beginning with a trio of basic pillows. The icons will rate the ease of the project, and the key on page 49 explains which skills are included in each category. As the projects progress, techniques are added so you'll have gained a repertoire of sewing skills by the end of the book. Once you understand a technique—adding an invisible zipper, for instance—you can apply it to just about any project. See pages 50 and 51 for a quick preview of each pillow.

**FOLLOW THE INSTRUCTIONS.** Purchase the fabric and notions according to our project instructions. We'll give you the directions that we used to make our pillows, including some witty commentary along the way. Our how-to photography will make it a breeze to follow the instructions.

**PREPARE TO SEW.** Now that you've got everything you need to begin making your pillow, arrange your tools and materials within easy reach. There's nothing worse than squinting while you're sewing, so treat yourself to adequate lighting in your workspace.

Speaking of tools and materials, you'll see a list for each of our pillow projects. However, we're not going to list every single little supply you need for each pillow, but rather refer you to this list of basic tools and materials. So, have the following on hand for any simply irresistible project in our Make a Pillow! section:

sewing machine

machine needles

measuring tools

marking tools

scissors

seam ripper

pins

needles for hand sewing

thread

point turner

iron

ironing board

Before you start to sew, repeat your mantra—$\frac{1}{2}$ inch seams, unless otherwise noted.

*Only a few more pages of handy information and our pillow talk will be over. Then, we'll spring into action and make lots of fabulous pillows.*

# Anatomy of a *Pillow*

## It's so easy to make a pillow. Who knew?

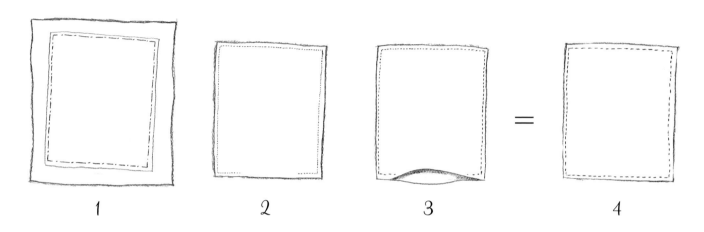

1          2          3          4

1 Cut out two pieces, one for the front and one for the back, that are the same size as your pillow form plus one inch in each dimension.

2 Place the right sides together and stitch the front to the back in a ½-inch seam, leaving an opening in one side.

3 Turn right side out and top-stitch around three sides. Stuff with fluff.

4 Complete the lines of stitching.

*Voilà! Your first pillow is complete. Enjoy.*

# Icon Key

Each of our projects is rated according to ease of construction. (Please note that I didn't say *difficulty* of construction.) Here's how we've organized them.

**ABSOLUTE BEGINNER**

*Suitable for the first-time sewer.*

**BASIC SKILLS YOU'LL USE:**

Pivot (page 27)

Trim seams and clip curves (page 28)

Right sides together (page 31)

Make a narrow hem (page 31)

Add a closure (page 32)

Make a flange (page 33)

Add a facing (page 39)

**EASY BEGINNER**

*Suitable for the new sewer who understands the basics and is ready to add a zipper.*

**NEW SKILLS YOU'LL USE:**

Install a centered zipper (page 35)

Install an invisible zipper (page 37)

**EXPERIENCED BEGINNER**

*Suitable for the sewer who's mastered the zipper and is ready to redecorate the neighborhood.*

**NEW SKILLS YOU'LL USE:**

Make piping (page 39)

Add a boxing strip (page 42)

## Tip
A tip offers you a nifty idea.

## Why?
Wondering why you're doing something? Here's the answer.

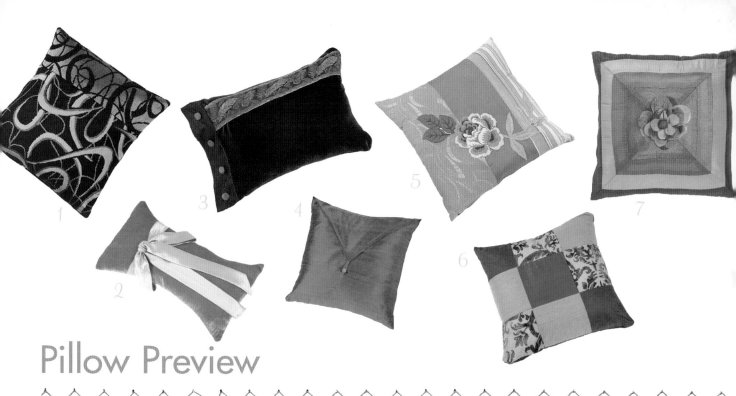

# Pillow Preview

*Here's the skinny on the pillows you'll see in the pages ahead. Aren't they great?*

1 **SIMPLE COLLECTION**
Take a simple shape to new places with some cool reversible fabric.

2 **GIFT-WRAPPED PILLOWS**
A little velvet goes a long way, especially when it's presented in a beautiful package.

3 **ZEN FLANGE PILLOWS**
Marry some sophisticated fabrics to create these stylish pillows.

4 **ALL BUTTONED UP**
Buttons as embellishment? Wait 'til you see these sparkle on shiny silk dupioni.

5 **FLORAL FANTASY**
This pillow is practically blooming with excitement, as a mixture of fabrics creates a virtual garden.

6 **BOHEMIAN PATCHWORK PILLOWS**
A traditional technique can yield very contemporary results, as you'll see in these pillows made from (just a little bit!) of luxurious fabric.

7 **BLOOMING GEOMETRY**
Even if you hated geometry, you'll love this striking pillow with a sweet flower accent.

**8  TIBETAN OPULENCE**
Play with fur (the fake kind, of course) and rich brocade in this homage to the Orient.

**9  POP ART PILLOWS**
Have some fun with coordinating fabrics as you add piping to a pillow that's really fun.

**10  PROUDLY ROUND**
You guessed it—these pillows are round and really interesting, featuring some unexpected fabrics.

**11  SPRING GARDEN SET**
If you're a nature lover, get ready to fall for these appliquéd pillows.

**12  BIG BANG PILLOWS**
Want to send your sofa into orbit? Make a funky pillow that features appliqués *and* embroidery.

**13  COLLAGE PILLOW**
Experiment with decorative elements such as beaded trim and sequins to create a piece of pillow art.

**14  EDGY BOLSTERS**
Pillows don't have to be square, you know. These bolsters feature exposed seams and cool ribbon decoration.

**15  NOT-SO-CRAZY QUILT PILLOW**
Not only it is *not* crazy, it's beautiful. Assemble a distinctive collection of fabric and trim for this stylish pillow.

*Can't decide?
Make all three.*

ABSOLUTE BEGINNER

Cheat sheet for absolute
beginner on page 49

# $\mathcal{S}$imple Collection

*Use a variety of easy construction techniques to make this trio of cool pillows.*

## Modern Knife-Edge Pillow

### WHAT YOU NEED

Basic pillow-making tools & supplies

Approximately ½ yard of reversible chenille fabric

14 x 14-inch pillow form

Thread to match the chenille fabric

### FINISHED SIZE

Approximately 14 x 14 inches

### HOW YOU MAKE IT

1 For the pillow front, cut two pieces of chenille, one that's 5½ x 15 inches and another that's 10½ x 15 inches. Cut the smaller strip from the reverse side of the fabric. Place these pieces right sides together and stitch in a double-stitched seam (photo 1). Trim the seam and press to one side.

2 For the pillow back, cut a piece of chenille that's 20½ x 15 inches. Cut this piece in half, making two pieces that are each 10¼ x 15 inches. Turn under ¼ inch on the edges you just cut and press; turn under 1 inch on these edges and stitch (photo 2).

3 Place the front right side up. Place one side of the back onto the front, right sides facing, with the raw edges even and the hemmed edge in the

Photo 1

Photo 2

Photo 3

center. Overlap the remaining back piece, right side down, with hemmed edge in the center. Pin in place (photo 3).

4 Stitch around all four sides. Reinforce the stitching at the corners and trim each corner. Turn inside out and insert the pillow form.

# Reversible Pillow

### WHAT YOU NEED

Basic pillow-making tools & supplies

Approximately ½ yard of reversible chenille fabric

Approximately ½ yard of contrasting fabric

Polyester fiberfill

Thread to match the chenille fabric and the contrasting fabric

### FINISHED SIZE

Approximately 14¼ x 14¼ inches

### HOW YOU MAKE IT

1 Cut two pieces that are each 15 x 15 inches, one from the chenille and the other from the contrasting fabric.

2 With right sides together, stitch together in a 3/8-inch seam (photo 4), leaving a 6 to 8-inch opening in one side. Reinforce the corners and trim. Turn and press the open edges to the inside along the seamline.

3 Topstitch 1/4 inch from the three sewn edges (photo 5); this forms a mini-flange. (We used a different color thread in the bobbin, so the lines of stitching match the predominant color on each side. But please do what you want.) Stuff the inside with

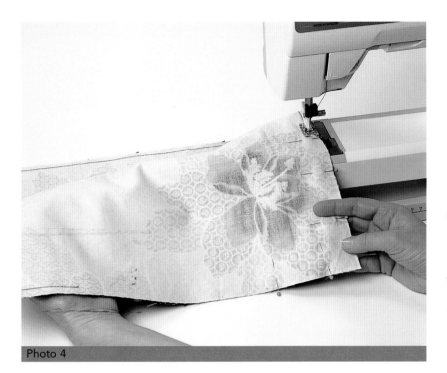
Photo 4

fiberfill as desired. Here's a tip—the more full you make the pillow, the more difficult it becomes to stitch it closed on the machine. Here's another tip—if you want to make your pillow pleasingly plump, stitch it together by hand instead of machine.

4 Pin together the open edges and topstitch, being sure to catch the folded edges.

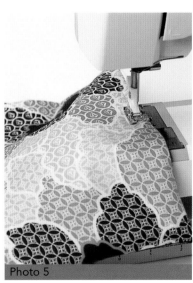
Photo 5

## Tie-End Pillow

**WHAT YOU NEED**

Basic pillow-making tools & supplies

Approximately ³⁄₈ yard of reversible chenille fabric

Approximately ¹⁄₄ yard of silk dupioni

Custom 10 x 16-inch pillow form

Thread to match the chenille fabric and the dupioni

**FINISHED SIZE**

Approximately 10 x 16 inches

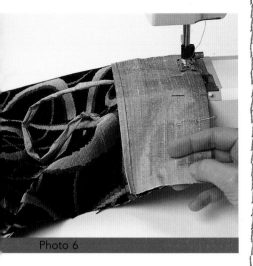
Photo 6

Photo 7

Photo 8

## HOW YOU MAKE IT

1 Cut one piece of chenille that's 11 x 33 inches. From the silk dupioni, cut two pieces that are each 4 x 11 inches (for the facing), and two pieces that are each 1½ x 18 inches (for the ties)

2 Make a narrow hem along one long edge of each facing piece, using matching thread.

3 Make two ties, using the method of your choice. We made tube ties, finished with a simple knot in one end. Baste one tie to the center of one of the short ends of the chenille piece, raw edges aligned. Baste the remaining tie to the center of the other short end.

4 Pin and stitch the facings to the short ends of the chenille piece, right sides together (photo 6). Be sure you don't catch the knotted ends of the ties in the stitching. Trim the seam and press toward the facings.

5 With right sides together and the facings extended (photo 7), pin and stitch the pillow. Turn the facings to the inside and press. Pin and stitch in the ditch, securing the facings to the side seams (photo 8).

6 Insert the pillow form, tucking the end under one side of the facing (photo 9). Read about making a custom pillow form on page 43, in case you've forgotten.

Photo 9

# Gift-Wrapped Pillows

*Give the gift of comfort with these velvet pillows, wrapped up in shimmering charmeuse.*

Gift and package, all in one!

ABSOLUTE BEGINNER

Cheat sheet for absolute beginner on page 49

**WHAT YOU NEED**

- Basic pillow-making tools & supplies
- Approximately 1/2 yard of silk dupioni
- Approximately 1/2 yard of velvet
- Approximately 1/4 yard of charmeuse
- Polyester fiberfill
- Matching thread
- Template, page 111

**FINISHED SIZE**

Approximately 7 x 16 inches

## HOW YOU MAKE IT

1 Using the template, cut the front out of the velvet, and cut the back from the silk. To do this, place the line on the template along the lengthwise grain of the fabric. It should be parallel to the selvage. Measure from each arrow and tweak until each one is the same distance from the selvage. After cutting, transfer the placement marks for the ties to the silk piece (photo 1); we clipped them.

2 To make the ties, cut the charmeuse in half to form two long strips. Fold each piece lengthwise, right sides together, and pin. Trim each piece to about 30 inches long, then cut one end of each piece at an angle. Stitch this end, pivot, and continue along the long edge (photo 2). Turn each piece right side out through the unstitched end and press.

3 Pin each tie between the marks on the right side of the silk piece, matching raw edges (photo 3). Baste. Pin the velvet to the silk, right sides together, making sure not to catch the ties. Use lots of pins, as the nap of velvet can be a little slippery. Stitch, leaving an opening about 4 inches wide on one of the shorter sides.

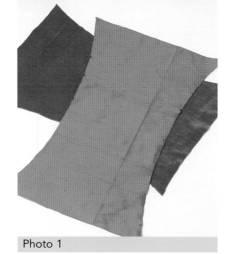

Photo 1

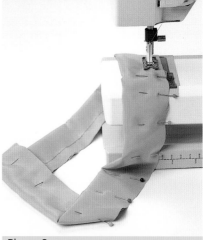

Photo 2

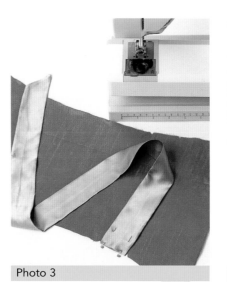

Photo 3

Photo 4

4 Stuff the pillow with fiber-fill, pushing it into the corners using a long tool, such as a wooden spoon (photo 4). To avoid creating clumps of batting, shred sections of it before stuffing. Push the batting gently into place.

5 Hand stitch the seam closed. Wrap and tie as desired.

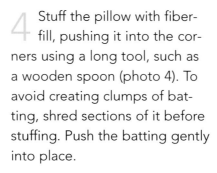

### Tip
**Pressing velvet will crush the nap. Instead, steam seams by holding the iron an inch away from the fabric, then finger press the seams open.**

# Zen Flange
# Pillows

*If you need to contemplate beauty, look no further than these elegant pillows.*

*Comfort. Beauty. Tranquility.*

**EASY BEGINNER**

Cheat sheet for easy beginner on page 49

# Side Flange Pillow

## HOW YOU MAKE IT

1 For the pillow front and back, cut two pieces of velvet that are each 15 x 19 inches. For the flange, cut two pieces of the contrasting fabric that are each 4 x 15 inches.

2 Make a narrow hem along one long edge of each piece of the flange (photo 1). Mark four buttonholes on one piece of the flange, about 1½ to 2 inches from the edge of the fabric and about 3½ inches apart from center to center (photo 2).

3 Refer to your sewing machine's manual and follow the instructions for making the buttonholes at the marked spots (photo 3). Cut the buttonholes open.

## WHAT YOU NEED

Basic pillow-making tools & supplies

Approximately ⅝ yard of velvet fabric

Approximately ⅛ yard of contrasting fabric for the flange

14 x 18-inch pillow form

Matching thread

Silk pins (optional)

Approximately ¾ yard of decorative trim

4 covered buttons, ¾ inch wide

## FINISHED SIZE

Approximately 14 x 18 inches

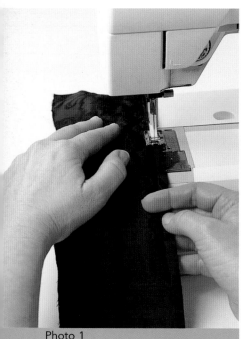

Photo 1

Photo 2

Photo 3

Photo 4

Photo 5

Photo 6

4 Cut a piece of decorative trim to the length of the pillow, which is 19 inches. Place the trim about 2 inches from the top of the pillow and pin carefully (photo 4). Stitch in place along each edge.

5 With right sides together, pin and stitch a flange piece to one end of each velvet piece (photo 5).

6 With right sides together, pin and stitch around the sides of the pillow *except* the flange end. We used round corners on this pillow. You may find that the velvet is easier to work with by stitching the square corners first, and then marking and stitching the round corners (photo 6).

7 Mark the button placement on the wrong side of the piece of flange that doesn't have the buttonholes. You'll stitch the buttons to the wrong side, so they'll button through the button-holes onto the right side of the pillow front, as you see on the opposite page.

8 Following the button manufacturer's instructions, cover the buttons with fabric as desired. (We used the contrasting fabric B from the Wrapped Pillow on the next page.) Sew the buttons to the flange. Insert the pillow form.

# Wrapped Pillow

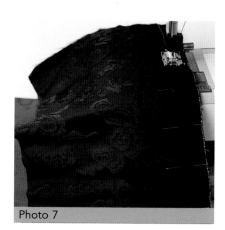

## WHAT YOU NEED

Basic pillow-making tools & supplies

Approximately ⅝ yard of velvet fabric for the pillow

Approximately ¼ yard of contrasting fabric A for the flange

Approximately ½ yard of contrasting fabric B for the wrap

18 x 18-inch pillow form

Matching thread

Silk pins (optional)

Approximately ½ yard of decorative trim

4 covered buttons, ¾ inch wide

20-inch invisible zipper

## FINISHED SIZE

Approximately 14 x 18 inches

## HOW YOU MAKE IT

1 For the pillow front and back, cut two pieces of velvet that are each 19 x 19 inches. For the wrap, cut a piece of fabric that's 13 x 31 inches; for the flange, cut two pieces of fabric that are each 6 x 13 inches.

2 Mark four buttonholes on the right side of one piece of the flange, about 2¼ inches from the edge of fabric and about 2 inches apart. Make the buttonholes as you did in step 3 on page 60.

3 With right sides together, pin and stitch the flange pieces to the ends of the wrap (photo 7).

4 Center the decorative trim over the seam between the flange and the wrap, placing it at the end of the wrap opposite the buttonholes. Pin and stitch in place (photo 8).

Photo 7

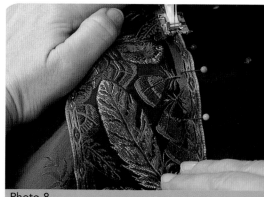

Photo 8

Photo 9

5 Make a narrow hem around all the raw edges.

6 Mark the spots for the buttons and sew them on. Here's the finished wrap (photo 9).

7 Make the pillow itself by first inserting an invisible zipper in one of the seams. Remember to install the invisible zipper before any seams are sewn. The right sides of the zipper tape should face the right sides of the fabric, with the zipper teeth at the seamline. Stitch each side of the zipper tape, using the invisible zipper foot. After installing the zipper, place the pillow front and back together, right sides facing, and use the regular zipper foot to finish the seam, starting above the last few stitches of the zipper installation.

8 Unzip the zipper. (If you don't unzip the zipper, you can't turn the pillow right side out!) With the right sides together, stitch the remaining three seams around the pillow. (As with the first pillow, this one has round corners.) Turn right side out through the opened zipper and stuff with the pillow form.

## Tips

We used silk and velvet for this oh-so-luxurious set of pillows. If you choose to use these luxe fabrics, be sure to pin carefully (and often!), as they can be slippery. It may be worth your time (not to mention money) to first practice on small swatches of material to get the feel for handling these fabrics. There are lots of silk-look synthetics, too.

You can use our wrap technique to give your rooms a quick makeover; they're fast and easy to sew, so you switch them out when you need some new eye candy.

# All Buttoned Up

These sophisticated pillows aren't afraid to have fun, with sparkly buttons and details from contrasting fabrics.

*A handsome pair, don't you think?*

**EASY BEGINNER**

Cheat sheet for easy beginner on page 49

# Green Envelope Flap

**HOW YOU MAKE IT**

1 Use the templates to cut out four pieces for this pillow—the front and the front facing (photo 1), and the back and the back facing (photo 2).

2 Make the loop closure just like the tie technique on page 35. Cut a strip of contrasting fabric that's 1 x 4½ inches. Fold it in half lengthwise and press; fold the raw edges to the inside, and press. Stitch. Fold it in half to create a loop and baste it to the right side of the point of the flap on the back, raw edges together (photo 3).

3 Make a ½-inch narrow hem on the bottom of the back facing and on one long edge of the front facing.

4 With right sides together, pin and stitch the front facing to the front. Also with right sides together, pin the back to the back facing and stitch together along the flap edges. Turn both pieces right sides out and press. Topstitch along the

Photo 1

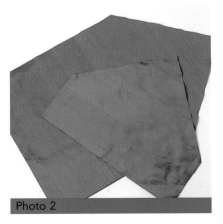

Photo 2

Photo 3

**WHAT YOU NEED**

Basic pillow-making tools & supplies

Approximately ¾ yard of silk dupioni

Approximately ⅛ yard of contrasting silk dupioni

12 x 12-inch pillow form

Thread to match both fabrics

Silk pins

1 button

Templates, page 111

**FINISHED SIZE**

Approximately 12 x 12 inches

**NOTE:** *Use ¼-inch seam allowances.*

Photo 4

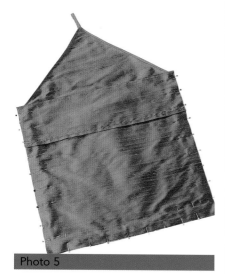

Photo 5

edges of the envelope flap (photo 4); topstitch across the top of the pillow where the flap meets the back. See the template for the placement of this stitching line.

5 With right sides together, pin the front to the back (photo 5), and then stitch the sides and bottom. Turn right side out and press. Insert the pillow form. Mark the placement of the button, remove the pillow form, and sew it in place.

# Scalloped Edge Pillow

## HOW YOU MAKE IT

1 Vary the template on page 111 to create a scalloped flap: from the topstitching line on the pattern, draw a rectangular flap that measures 7 x 13³/₄ inches. Use a compass or dressmaker's curve to draw the scallops. Make the same scalloped pattern on the facing, too.

2 Follow the directions in steps 2 through 5 on pages 65 and 66, making four loops to place on the four scalloped edges. Add four buttons as in step 5. Here's how the finished flap will look (photo 6).

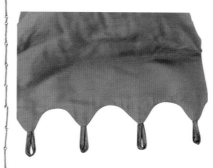

Photo 6

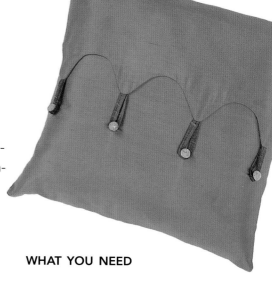

## WHAT YOU NEED

Basic pillow-making tools & supplies

Approximately ³/₄ yard of silk dupioni

Approximately ¹/₈ yard of contrasting silk dupioni

12 x 12-inch pillow form

Thread to match both fabrics

Silk pins

4 buttons

Templates, page 111

## FINISHED SIZE

Approximately 12 x 12 inches

## Why?

A pin is a pin, right? Not really. Silk pins have thin shafts and fine points, which leave less of a mark on fine silk fabrics. Invest in some silk pins to use when you're sewing with delicate material.

# Floral Fantasy

*For a little visual interest, mix and match fabrics for a couple of pillows that complement one another.*

**EASY BEGINNER**

Cheat sheet for easy beginner
on page 49

*Have a garden inside, all year long.*

# Big Flower Pillow

## HOW YOU MAKE IT

1 For the pillow back, cut a 17 x17-inch square from the tonal print fabric. For the front, cut the following panels: one piece of the tonal print fabric that's 7 x 17 inches; one piece of the silk that's 6 x17 inches; and one piece of the striped fabric that's 6 x17 inches.

2 With right sides together, pin and stitch the long sides of the front panel pieces, placing the silk panel in the center. Press the seams open (photo 1).

Photo 1

3 Look at the print fabric and choose a motif to use for the appliqué. (Be sure it will fit on the pillow, okay?) Cut it out of the fabric, leaving at least 1 inch around the motif. Now, cut a piece of the fusible web to the same size. Follow the manufacturer's instructions to apply the fusible web to the wrong side of the appliqué. Carefully cut away the excess fabric around the motif, leaving the paper in place on the back (photo 2). Remove the paper and iron the appliqué in place on the pillow front, again following the manufacturer's instructions.

Photo 2

## WHAT YOU NEED

Basic pillow-making tools & supplies

Approximately ¹/₂ yard of floral print fabric

Approximately ¹/₂ yard of tonal print fabric, in a shade to complement the floral print fabric

Approximately ¹/₄ yard of dupioni silk, in a shade to complement the print fabrics

Approximately ¹/₄ yard of striped fabric, in shades to complement the print fabrics

16 x 16-inch pillow form

Matching thread and clear nylon thread

Paper-backed fusible web

14-inch zipper

## FINISHED SIZE

Approximately 16 x 16 inches

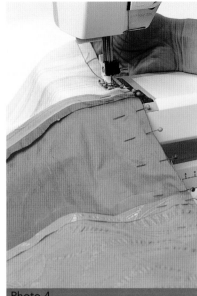

Photo 3

Photo 4

# Knife-Edge Flower Pillow

## WHAT YOU NEED

Basic pillow-making tools & supplies

Approximately ½ yard of floral print fabric

Approximately ½ yard of striped fabric, in a shade to complement the print fabric

14 x 14-inch pillow form

Matching thread

12-inch zipper

## FINISHED SIZE

Approximately 14 x 14 inches

4 With matching thread in the bobbin and clear nylon thread in the top, zigzag around the edge of the appliqué (photo 3)—set the zigzag stitch to a medium width and a very short length (a satin stitch). The satin stitch will keep the raw edges from raveling.

5 With right sides together, pin and stitch one side of the pillow front to one side of the pillow back, inserting a centered zipper in the seam. Install the zipper by stitching each end of the seam (photo 4), then basting the rest of the seam. Press the seam open. Place the zipper facedown over the basted part of the seam and baste in place with the zipper foot. Turn right side up and stitch in place. Remove the basting stitches.

6 Unzip the zipper (don't forget!). With right sides together, pin and stitch the remaining three seams around the pillow. Turn right side out through the opened zipper and stuff with the pillow form.

## HOW YOU MAKE IT

1 For the pillow front and back, cut two 15 x 15-inch squares from the print fabric. For the little flange, cut enough 2-inch bias strips to equal 60 inches when pieced and sewn together. Without pressing, fold the bias strip in half lengthwise, with the wrong sides facing. Baste the folded fabric together 1/4 inch from the raw edges (photo 5).

2 Place the flange strip on the right side of the front of the pillow, with the raw edges even. Pin if necessary. Baste the strip in place (photo 6), beginning about 3 inches from the end of the strip. Ease the flange strip around the corners. When you've stitched almost all the way to the beginning, stop stitching about three inches from the end.

3 Make a seam in the flange like so: join the ends of the flange and mark or pin in place (photo 7). Trim the excess flange, leaving a 1/2-inch seam allowance. Remove enough basting stitches so you can place the two ends together, right sides facing, and stitch together at the marked spot (photo 8). Turn and re-do the

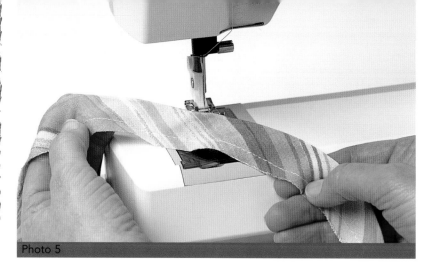
Photo 5

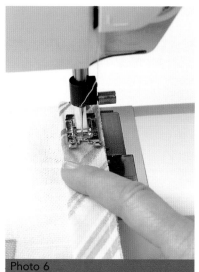
Photo 6

Photo 7

Photo 8

fold; your flange should now fit the pillow, and you can finish basting the flange to the pillow front.

4 Now you'll insert a zipper, pretty much the same way as in step 5 of the Big Flower Pillow, but there's a notable exception. It takes a lot of words to explain it, but it's really quite easy.

Your line of stitching has to start and stop at the seam, because the flange is hanging out there in the middle. Here's how to do this: when you baste the zipper in place, be sure to fold the flange to the opposite side while you're stitching, so it doesn't get caught. Do the same when you're stitching the zipper in place. After you pivot, stitch right up to the seam and backstitch (photo 9). Take the needle out of the fabric and lift the presser foot. Start stitching again on the other side of the flange, after you fold it to the side you just stitched (photo 10). You may want to mark the spot to start stitching, so it's even with the other side. (We did, using a pin.) After you've begun your line of stitching, backstitch a couple of stitches to secure the seam.

5 Unzip the zipper. With the right sides together, pin and stitch the remaining three seams around the pillow. Turn right side out through the opened zipper and stuff with the pillow form.

Photo 9

Photo 10

> ## Why?
> Why do you have to put a zipper in the Knife-Edge Flower Pillow? You don't! If step 4 seems scary, simply omit the zipper. After you've completed step 3, place the right sides together and stitch around all four sides of the pillow, leaving a 6-inch opening. Turn the pillow right side out, stuff with fiberfill, and slipstitch closed.

# Bohemian Patchwork Pillows

*Add an elegant touch to any room with these boho works of art.*

*The perfect pillow for your beautiful free spirit.*

**EASY BEGINNER**

Cheat sheet for easy beginner on page 49

# Square Pillow

## HOW YOU MAKE IT

1 For the front, cut nine squares that are each 7 x 7 inches, using all four of the fabrics (photo 1). For the back, cut one piece that's 19 x 19 inches.

2 Organize the squares into your desired pattern. To keep the squares stable when you stitch them, you may want to apply fusible interfacing to the wrong side of each square, as we did here (photo 2). Follow the manufacturer's instructions to apply the interfacing. With right sides together, pin and stitch the squares into three strips, with three squares in each strip (photo 3). Press open the seam allowances.

Photo 1

Photo 2

Photo 3

## WHAT YOU NEED

Basic pillow-making tools & supplies

Approximately ¼ yard of four different fabrics for the pillow front (we used silk dupioni, silk jacquard, and silk devore)

Approximately ⅝ yard of silk dupioni for the pillow back

18 x18-inch pillow form

Matching thread

Fusible interfacing (optional)

20-inch invisible zipper

## FINISHED SIZE

Approximately 18 x 18 inches

Photo 4

3 With right sides facing, carefully pin one strip to a second strip, matching the seams from step 2. (To check the alignment, place a pin in the ditch of the seams you're matching, as shown in photo 4.) Stitch. Repeat to stitch together the third strip. Press open the seam allowances.

4 After you've created the patchwork front, sew the invisible zipper in the bottom seam. Remember to install the invisible zipper before any seams are sewn. The right sides of the zipper tape should face the right sides of the fabric, with the zipper teeth at the seamline. Stitch each side of the zipper tape, using the invisible zipper foot. After installing the zipper, place the pillow front and back together, right sides facing, and use the regular zipper foot to finish the bottom seam, starting above the last few stitches of the zipper installation.

5 Unzip the zipper. (If you don't unzip the zipper, you can't turn the pillow right side out!) With the right sides together, pin and stitch the remaining three seams around the pillow. (This pillow has round corners.) Turn right side out through the opened zipper and stuff with the pillow form.

## Why?

What's up with the fusible inter-facing? Some of the fabrics we used in this project, particularly the devore, are flimsy. The interfacing acts as a stabilizing layer and makes the silk much easier to sew. If you're not using slippery fabrics for your pillow, you probably won't need the interfacing.

# Rectangle Pillow

### WHAT YOU NEED

Basic pillow-making tools & supplies

Approximately 1/4 yard of four different fabrics for the front (we used silk dupioni, silk jacquard, and silk devore)

Approximately 5/8 yard of silk dupioni for the back

14 x18-inch pillow form

Matching thread

Fusible interfacing (optional)

20-inch invisible zipper

### FINISHED SIZE

Approximately 14 x 18 inches

1 For the pillow front, cut nine squares that are each 5$\frac{3}{4}$ x 7 inches, using all four of the fabrics. For the back, cut one piece that's 15 x 19 inches.

2 Construct as the Square Pillow, steps 2 through 5.

# Blooming Geometry

*Even if you hate math, you'll love this orderly design.*

*Work all the angles by displaying either the front or the back.*

 **EASY BEGINNER**

Cheat sheet for easy beginner on page 49

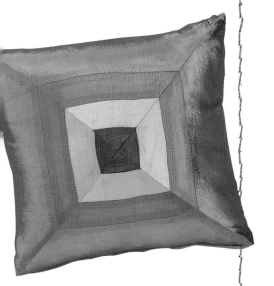

Photo 1

Photo 2

## WHAT YOU NEED

Basic pillow-making tools & supplies

Approximately 1 yard each of four different fabrics

16 x 16-inch pillow form

Matching thread

Scrap paper

Templates, page 111

Freezer paper

Fray retardant (optional)

Batting or fiberfill

16-inch zipper

## FINISHED SIZE

Approximately 16 x 16 inches

## HOW YOU MAKE IT

1 For the front and the back, cut four pieces from one of the fabrics that are each $4^{1}/_{2}$ x 34 inches. Cut four pieces from each of the remaining three fabrics that are each $2^{1}/_{2}$ x 34 inches.

2 With right sides facing, pin and stitch the fabric strips together, with the wider piece at the bottom.

Photo 3

Repeat to make four strips. Press all the seams open (photo 1).

3 Make a triangle template that's 12 x 12 x 17 inches. Use this template to cut out triangles from the fabric strips (photo 2): cut four triangles with the wide strip at the bottom, and then reverse the template to cut out four triangles with a narrow strip at the bottom. You'll get three triangles from each strip, two in the same orientation and one in the opposite orientation. (You'll have a few leftover triangles.)

4 Make the pillow front from the four triangles with the narrow strip at the bottom. With right sides together, pin and stitch two of the triangles together, matching the seams. Repeat to stitch the remaining two triangles together (photo 3). With right sides together, stitch the pair of triangles together. Make the pillow back as above, by using the triangles with the wide strip at the bottom.

Photo 4

5 Trace or copy the templates on page 111 and cut them out. Cut out three pieces of the freezer paper that are each about 12 x 12 inches. Apply the pieces of the freezer paper to three of the fabrics; dry-iron the waxy side to the fabric. Use the templates to trace and cut out two flowers of each size per color (photo 4). Remove the freezer paper. Apply fray retardant to the edges of the flowers if desired.

6 To make the flower center, cut a 3-inch circle from one of the fabrics. Place a small bit of batting in the center of the circle, gather the fabric around it, and hand stitch together. Layer the flowers as desired, alternating the colors. Tack tightly in the center, so the completed blossom springs up a bit. Stitch the flower center in place. Stitch the flower into the center of the pillow.

7 With right sides together, pin and stitch one side of the pillow front to one side of the pillow back, inserting a centered zipper in the seam. Install the zipper by stitching each end of the seam to the appropriate spot, then basting the middle of the seam. Press the seam open. Place the zipper facedown over the middle of the seam and baste in place with the zipper foot. Turn right side up and stitch in place. Remove the basting stitches.

8 Unzip the zipper (don't forget!). With right sides together, pin and stitch the remaining three seams around the pillow. Turn right side out through the opened zipper and stuff with the pillow form.

## Why?
The freezer paper makes it much easier to cut out the flowers, as it gives the fabric a bit more body.

EXPERIENCED BEGINNER

Cheat sheet for experienced
beginner on page 49

*Don't be afraid to
curl up with this
magnificent pillow!*

# Tibetan Opulence

*Fit for a queen, this pillow features several different fabrics that exude luxury and a bit of mystery, too.*

## HOW YOU MAKE IT

1 For the pillow front and the pillow back, cut two pieces of brocade that are each 19 x 13 inches, and cut two pieces of fur that are each 19 x 7 inches. For the inner flap, cut two pieces of brocade that are each 10 x 18 inches. For the lining, cut two pieces of fabric that are each 19 x 7 inches.

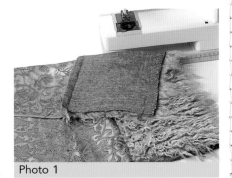
Photo 1

2 With right sides together, pin each of the 19 x 13-inch pieces of brocade to a piece of fur along the long edge. Stitch (photo 1).

Photo 2

3 Cut a piece of trim that's 19 inches long. Pin the trim to one of the pieces of brocade, about 1 inch from the faux fur. Stitch in place along both edges. This piece will be the pillow front.

4 Now make the inner flap. With right sides together, pin the two pieces together and stitch along three sides, leaving open one of the long sides. Trim the corners, turn right side out, press, and topstitch close to the three stitched edges (photo 2).

5 Cut the leather cord into four equal pieces. Baste two of the cords onto the long edge of each piece of lining, placing the cords on the right side of the fabric and equidistant from the end. The end of the cord should be flush with the edge of the lining.

## WHAT YOU NEED

Basic pillow-making tools & supplies

Approximately 1 yard of brocade

Approximately ¼ yard of faux fur

Approximately ¼ yard of lining fabric, in a contrasting color

16 x 16-inch pillow form

Matching thread

Approximately 1 yard of leather cord

Approximately ⅝ yard of trim

4 Asian coins

## FINISHED SIZE

Approximately 18 x 18 inches

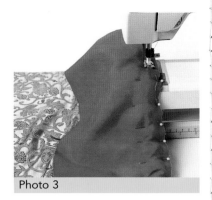

Photo 3

Photo 4

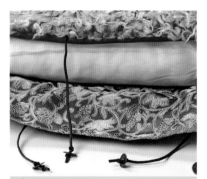

Photo 5

Photo 6

6 With right sides together, pin each piece of lining to the faux fur; make sure the cords are between the two layers of fabric. Stitch (photo 3). On the right side of one of the lining pieces, center and pin the long raw edge of the flap (photo 4). There should be an inch or so of lining on either side of the flap. Stitch and press the seam toward the lining. Finish the raw edge of the other piece of lining, using a narrow hem or a zigzag stitch.

7 Open out the lining. With right sides facing, pin the pillow front and back together, matching seams. Stitch the three sides, making certain not to catch the flap in the seams. Trim the corners and tack the lining fabric to the seam allowances to keep it in place. Turn the pillow right side out.

8 Slip a coin onto each leather cord, tying a knot on either side of the coins to keep them near the ends of the cords. Here's the finished pillow, with the pillow form inside (photo 5). Fold the flap over the pillow form and tie the cords to close (photo 6).

## Tips

Here are a few suggestions when working with faux fur.

When pinning it, push (or pull, whatever) the furry fibers away from the edge of the fabric as best you can, so they won't be stitched into the seam. Use your fingers (or a pin) to pull out and fluff any naughty fibers that are caught in the stitching. Because pressing could melt the fur, first finger-press any seams, and then steam the wrong side, holding the iron a few inches away from the fabric. You may have to baste your seams, depending on the thickness of your faux fur.

# Pop Art Pillows

*Find some mind-blowing fabric to make this set of groovy pillows.*

*Make them both, just for kicks.*

EXPERIENCED BEGINNER

Cheat sheet for experienced beginner on page 49

# Floor Pillow

### HOW YOU MAKE IT

1 For the pillow front and back, cut two 25 x 25-inch squares; we used different fabrics for the front and back. Cut enough 1⅝-inch bias strips to make two 98-inch-long piping strips when pieced and sewn together; again, we used different fabrics for each 98-inch strip. Cut two pieces for the boxing strip, one piece that's 6 x 49 inches and one piece that's 5 x 49 inches. Cut the 6-inch piece in half lengthwise and install a centered zipper in this piece.

Install the zipper by placing the right sides together and stitching each end of the seam to the appropriate spot, then basting the middle of the seam. Press the seam open. Place the zipper facedown over the middle of the seam and baste in place with the zipper foot. Turn right side up and stitch in place. Remove the basting stitches.

2 Pin and stitch the short ends of the boxing strip together, right sides facing. Press the seams open. Place the strip around the foam for fit, adjusting if necessary, because sometimes the foam pieces may not be cut just exactly perfect. Or sometimes your sewing may not be exactly perfect! Center the zipper across one side and mark the four corners of the boxing strip (photo 1).

## WHAT YOU NEED

Basic pillow-making tools & supplies

Approximately 1½ yards of 54-inch floral print fabric for the pillow front

Approximately 1½ yards of 54-inch polka dot fabric, in a coordinating color to the floral print fabric, for the pillow back

Approximately ½ yard of 54-inch striped fabric for the boxing strip, in shades that complement the print fabrics

4-inch-wide foam, cut to 24 x 24 inches

Matching thread

30-inch zipper

6 yards of ½-inch diameter cording

Fiberfill or batting (optional)

## FINISHED SIZE

Approximately 24 x 24 inches

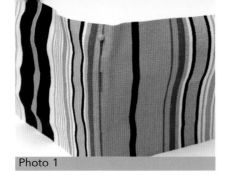

Photo 1

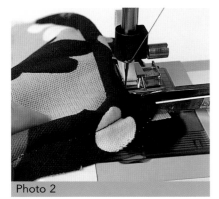

Photo 2

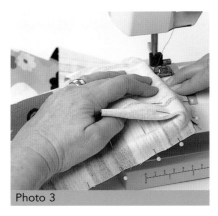

Photo 3

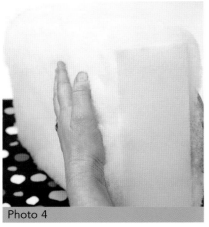

Photo 4

3 Sew together the bias strips, right sides together, forming two 98-inch strips. You're making them a few inches longer for peace of mind. (Remember that the pieces should be slightly offset, forming a right angle, when you stitch them to one another with the right sides facing.) As with the pillow front and back, we used contrasting fabric for each bias strip—we made strips from the fabric we used for the pillow back and put them on the pillow front, and vice versa. Fold each strip together, wrong sides facing, and encase the cording in the middle. Stitch as close to the cording as you can, using your zipper foot. (Aren't those zipper feet handy?)

4 Use the zipper foot to baste one strip to the pillow front, beginning in the center of one side. Begin stitching 1 inch from the end of the strip, sewing as close to the cording as you can. (Align the strips at the fabric edge, because they were designed to leave a perfect ½-inch seam allowance after the cording was encased.) As you reach the corners, clip the strip to fit (photo 2). If you need to pin the piping first, feel free, but it's easy to line up the edges and stitch.

5 When you're a couple of inches away from finishing, stop with the needle in the fabric. Rip out enough stitches to uncover the cording at either end and trim it so the ends are flush. Fold under one end of the fabric and cover the other end of the strip. Complete the line of stitching to sew the piping in place. Repeat to baste the remaining bias strip onto the pillow back.

6 With the right sides together, pin the boxing strip to the pillow front, matching the corners. Stitch in place, clipping the strip to fit around the corners as you did in step 4 (photo 3). Unzip the zipper and then stitch the boxing strip to the pillow back. (If you don't unzip the zipper, you can't turn the pillow right side out!)

7 Turn the pillow right side out. If desired, add a layer of batting around the foam for a softer, fuller pillow (photo 4), and insert into the pillow cover.

## WHAT YOU NEED

Basic pillow-making tools & supplies

2 coordinating fabrics for the pillow front and back, approximately ½ yard of each

Matching thread

Fiberfill

## FINISHED SIZE:

Approximately 11 x 11 inches

### Why?

Due to the size of the Floor Pillow, it's best to use fabrics that are 54 inches wide. If you use three different fabrics for these pillows, you'll have some material left over. Make something cool with it!

# Mock Box Pillow

## HOW YOU MAKE IT

1 For the pillow front and back, cut two pieces that are each 15-inch squares; we used different fabrics for the front and back just as we did for the Floor Pillow. With right sides facing, pin and stitch the pillow front to the pillow back, leaving a 6-inch opening on one side.

Photo 5

2 Press the seams open. Align the seams at the corner; to help align them, place a pin horizontally above the fold and turn inside out. Check the alignment, adjust if necessary, and secure by placing a pin in the ditch through the aligned seams; it should be in the center of each seam. In photo 5, you'll see how both of these pins are used to align the seams. (No, we didn't use the pins at the same time, silly. Just trying to save a little film.)

Photo 6

3 Measure from the corner and mark a line that's half the depth of the pillow; in this case, the 3-inch-deep pillow was marked 1½ inches from the corner (busy photo 5 again). Stitch across the marked line. Repeat for each corner. Turn inside out (photo 6).

4 Stuff the pillow with fiberfill and slipstitch the opening.

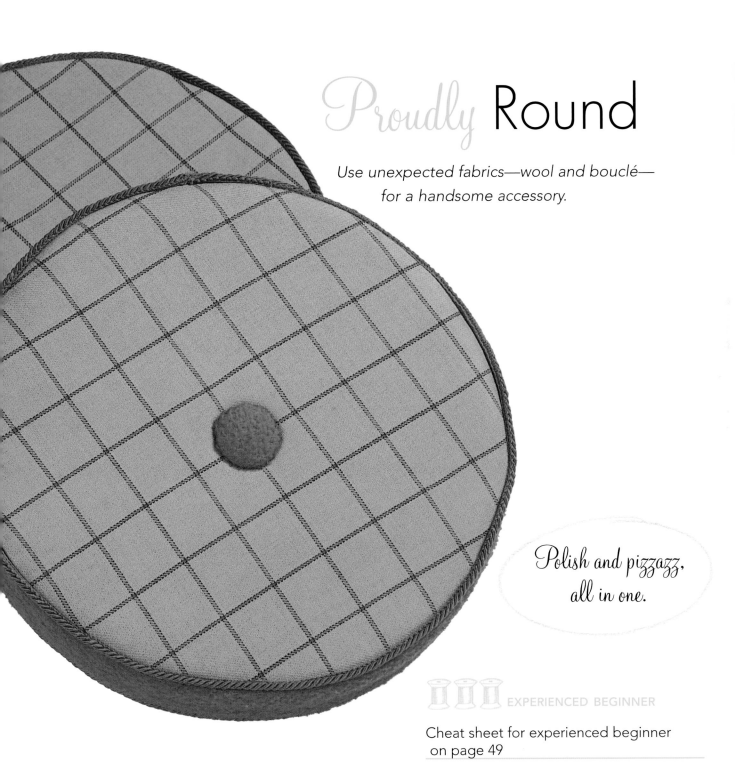

# Proudly Round

*Use unexpected fabrics—wool and bouclé—
for a handsome accessory.*

*Polish and pizzazz,
all in one.*

EXPERIENCED BEGINNER

Cheat sheet for experienced beginner
on page 49

## WHAT YOU NEED

Basic pillow-making tools & supplies

Approximately ½ yard of plaid fabric for the pillow front and back

Approximately ⅜ yard of bouclé fabric for the boxing strip and the covered buttons

14 x 2-inch round foam rubber pillow form

Matching thread

Fabric marking pen

9-inch zipper

Approximately 3 yards of braided trim

2 half-ball covered buttons, 1½ inches

Upholstery (heavy-duty) thread

Upholstery needle

## FINISHED SIZE

Approximately 14 inches in diameter

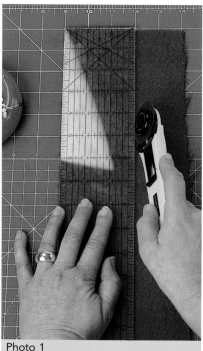

Photo 1

Photo 2

## HOW YOU MAKE IT

1 For the pillow front and back, trace around the pillow form to cut out two pieces of plaid fabric. Don't add an additional seam allowance, so the pillow will fit the foam tightly once it's inserted. (However, you should stitch all the seams with the standard 1/2-inch seam allowance. Take my word for it.) Cut three pieces for the boxing strip, one that's 3 x 36 inches, and two that are 2 x 14 inches (photo 1).

2 Pin the braided trim to the right side of each round piece of fabric, matching the raw edges, and trim to fit, allowing an extra inch on either end. Baste using the zipper foot, overlapping the ends into the seam allowance (photo 2).

Photo 3

Photo 4

Photo 5

3 Now you'll stitch the short pieces of the boxing strip together lengthwise, right sides together, and insert a centered zipper. Install the zipper by stitching each end of the seam to the appropriate spot, then basting the middle of the seam. Press the seam open. Place the zipper facedown over the middle of the seam and baste in place with the zipper foot. Turn right side up and stitch in place. Remove the basting stitches. Pin and stitch one end of the long boxing strip to one end of the strip with the zipper, right sides together.

4 Pin the boxing strip to the pillow front, right sides together; begin by turning one end of the boxing strip under 1/2 inch. When you get all the way around, you'll have some leftover boxing strip. Trim the strip and overlap the end (photo 3). Baste, again using a zipper foot. Stitch. Unzip the zipper and then stitch the boxing strip to the pillow back. (If you don't unzip the zipper, you can't turn the pillow right side out!)

5 Turn right side out. Stitch the overlapped seam closed by hand (photo 4). Fold and insert the pillow form; it will be a tight squeeze!

6 Follow the manufacturer's instructions to cover the buttons. Using an upholstery needle and heavy-duty thread, sew them to each other at the center of the pillow, stitching through the foam (photo 5).

*Please don't pick the flowers.*

**EXPERIENCED BEGINNER**

Cheat sheet for experienced beginner
on page 49

# Spring Garden Set

*These pillows blossom with a sprinkling of leaves and flowers.*

## Large Garden Pillow

### HOW YOU MAKE IT

1 For the pillow front, cut one piece of the sueded fabric that's a 15-inch square. For the pillow back, cut two pieces of the sueded fabric, one that's 12 x 15 inches and another that's 9½ x 15 inches. For the flange, cut eight pieces of the rayon fabric that are each 4 x 22 inches.

2 Use the templates to cut out an assortment of flowers and leaves from scrap paper. Cut out four pieces of the fusible web that are each 8 x 10 inches. Following the manufacturer's instructions, fuse three of these pieces onto each of the silk fabrics, and fuse the remaining piece onto the rayon fabric. Do not remove the paper backing after fusing; instead, use the templates to trace designs onto the paper backing, and then cut out the flowers and leaves (photo 1).

3 Arrange the cut pieces on the pillow front. (Do this on the ironing board, so you won't have to move your final design). Remove the paper backing and iron the pieces in position. With match-ing thread in the bobbin and clear nylon thread on top, zigzag all the way around each piece, using a medi-um width setting and very short stitch length. Using thread and needle, stitch the seed beads in position in the center of the flowers.

Photo 1

### WHAT YOU NEED

Basic pillow-making tools & supplies

Approximately ½ yard of sueded fabric for the pillow front and back

Approximately ¼ yard of rayon fabric for the flange

Approximately ⅛ yard each of three colors of dupioni silk for the appliqués

14 x 14-inch pillow form

Templates, page 111

Scrap paper

Paper-backed fusible web

Matching thread

Clear nylon thread

Black seed beads

Hand sewing needle

### FINISHED SIZE

Approximately 14 x 14 inches

4 For the pillow back, make an overlap (or sham) closure. Turn under ¼ inch on one of the 15-inch raw edges of each of the pieces, and then press under an additional 1¾ inches. Stitch in place. Overlap the pieces so they form a 15-inch square and baste the pieces together at the overlap, about ¼ inch from the edge.

5 Right sides together, pin a flange piece to one side of the pillow front. Center the flange strip so there's a 4-inch extension on each side. Stitch, beginning and ending ½ inch from each corner of the pillow front. Add the next piece by starting to stitch where the previous line of stitching ended (photo 2). Repeat this on all sides of the pillow front and the pillow back.

6 Make mitered corners by folding the excess flange at a 45° angle; pin to check the angle, if necessary (photo 3). Stitch from inner corner to outer corner (photo 4), and trim the seam. Press the seam open.

Photo 2

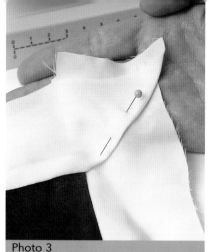
Photo 3

Photo 4

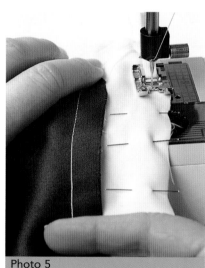
Photo 5

7 With right sides facing, pin the pillow front and back together and stitch all the way around the flange (photo 5). Trim the corners. Turn right side out through the overlap closure and press the flange. With matching thread, top-stitch all the way around the edge of the pillow (photo 6), through all layers, so it will encase the pillow form. Stuff the form through the closure.

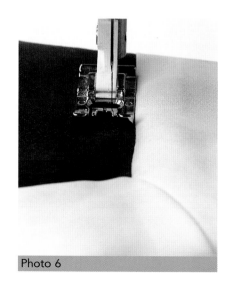
Photo 6

# Small Garden Pillow

## WHAT YOU DO

1 For the pillow front, cut one piece of the sueded fabric that's a 13-inch square. For the pillow back, cut two pieces of the sueded fabric, one that's 10½ x 13 inches and another that's 8 x 13 inches. For the flange, cut eight pieces of the rayon fabric that are each 2 inches by 17 inches.

2 Follow the instructions for the Large Garden Pillow, steps 2 through 7, but overlap the back pieces to form a 13-inch square in step 4. In step 5, you should have a 2-inch extension on each side.

## WHAT YOU NEED

Basic pillow-making tools & supplies

Approximately ½ yard of sueded fabric for the pillow front and back

Approximately ¼ yard of rayon fabric for the flange

Approximately ⅛ yard each of three colors of dupioni silk for the appliqués

12 x 12-inch pillow form

Templates, page 111

Scrap paper

Paper-backed fusible web

Matching thread

Clear nylon thread

Black seed beads

## FINISHED SIZE

Approximately 12 x 12 inches

# Big Bang Pillows

Create your own solar system, using funky fabrics and celestial felt appliqués.

*Your room will orbit around these cool pillows.*

**EXPERIENCED BEGINNER**

Cheat sheet for experienced beginner on page 49

# Satellite Pillow

## WHAT YOU NEED

Basic pillow-making tools & supplies

Approximately 1 yard of print fabric for the pillow front and back

Approximately ¼ yard each of three colors of felt to match the print

14 x 14 x 3-inch pillow form

Approximately 3½ yards of small string for piping

Matching thread

Clear nylon thread

1 skein of perle cotton (or embroidery floss)

Embroidery needle

Freezer paper (optional)

## FINISHED SIZE

Approximately 14 x 14 inches

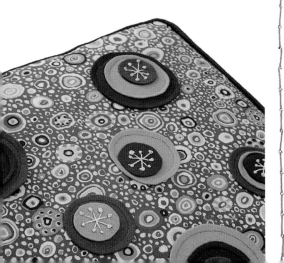

## HOW YOU MAKE IT

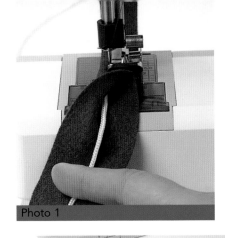
Photo 1

1 For the pillow front, cut a 15-inch square. For the pillow back, cut two pieces, one that's 10 x 15 inches, and another that's 13 x 15 inches. For the boxing strip, cut two pieces that are each 4 x 45 inches.

2 Choose one of the felt colors for the piping. Cut enough 1½-inch strips to make two 60-inch-long strips when pieced and sewn together; remember that the strips should be slightly off-set, forming a right angle,

Photo 2

when you stitch them to one another with the right sides facing. Press the seams open. Fold each strip together, wrong sides facing, and encase the string in the middle (photo 1). Stitch as close to the cording as you can, using your zipper foot. (Aren't those zipper feet handy?)

3 Cut circles of felt, in varying colors and sizes; ours are 3 inches, 2 inches, and 1½ inches in diameter. (If desired, dry-iron the waxy side of pieces of freezer paper to the felt and trace round objects onto the paper backing, then cut them out and remove the paper.) Arrange the circles on the front of the pillow, stacking them asymmetrically. Before attaching the circles to the pillow front, embellish the circles with embroidery. Stitch through the circles to the right side. Make a French knot, bring the needle back up beside the French knot, and make a long straight stitch to the opposite side. Make another French knot. Repeat this sequence on all the stacked circles to create a star shape (photo 2).

4 Pin the stacked circles onto the front of the pillow. With the matching thread in the bobbin and the clear nylon thread in the top, stitch around the bottommost circles (photo 3).

5 For the pillow back, make an overlap (or sham) closure. Turn under ¼ inch on one of the 15-inch raw edges of each of the pieces, and then press under an additional 1¾ inches. Stitch in place. Overlap the pieces so they form a 15-inch square and baste the pieces together at the overlap, about ¼ inch from the edge.

6 Use the zipper foot to sew one piping strip to the pillow front, beginning at the edge of the fabric in one corner (photo 4). Align the strips at the fabric edge, because they were designed to leave a perfect ½-inch seam allowance after the string was encased. As you reach the other corners, clip the strip to fit if necessary. If you need to pin the piping first, feel free, but it's easy to line up the edges and stitch. At the last corner, overlap the ends of the piping strip into the seam allowance. Repeat to sew the remaining piping strip onto the pillow back.

Photo 3

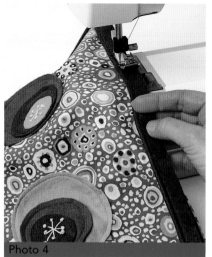
Photo 4

Photo 5

7 Pin and stitch one short end of the boxing strip together, right sides facing. Press the seam open. On either side of the seam, make two rows of basting stitches along both long edges, leaving 6 inches of thread at each end. Pull the threads to gather the piece until it measures 57 inches in length (photo 5). Tie knots in the threads to maintain the gathered length. Stitch the remaining short end together, right sides facing, keeping the gathering threads free.

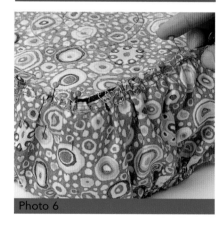
Photo 6

8 Pin the boxing strip to the pillow front, right sides together, placing the seams in the strip at opposite corners. Adjust the gathers, placing the pillow on the form if necessary (photo 6). Stitch, using a zipper foot. Repeat to stitch the boxing strip to the pillow back.

9 Turn right side out through the sham closing and stuff with the pillow form.

# Rings of Saturn Pillow

## WHAT YOU NEED

Basic pillow-making tools & supplies

Approximately ½ yard of print fabric for the pillow front and back

Approximately ⅛ yard each of three colors of felt to match the print

12 x 12-inch pillow form

Pen or knitting needle (optional)

## FINISHED SIZE

Approximately 12 x 12 inches

Photo 7

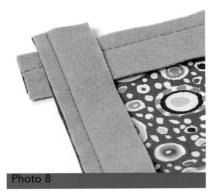
Photo 8

## WHAT YOU DO

1 For the pillow front, cut a 14-inch square. For the pillow back, cut two pieces, one that's 12 x 13 inches and one that's 9 x 13 inches. From each of the colors of felt, cut four pieces that are each 1¼ x 13 inches.

2 Make a sham closing for the back as in step 5 of the Satellite Pillow, turning under one of the edges of the 13-inch pieces. The back pieces should overlap to form a 13-inch square.

3 To make the felt edging, stack the felt pieces atop the other, but stagger them so they're ¼ inch apart. Baste them together 1 inch from the bottom edge. Mark 1¼ inch from the bottom edge and trim the entire strip to this measurement (photo 7). Repeat for the remaining three strips.

4 Turn the strips upside down, so the widest piece of felt is on top. Now, place each strip along the pillow front, with the stacked edge to the raw edge of the pillow front. At the corners, the felt pieces will overlap (photo 8); alternate which piece is on the top. Pin and baste.

5 With right sides together, pin and stitch the pillow front to the pillow back. Clip the corners, and turn right side out through the sham closing. You may need a tool (like a pen or a knitting needle) to gently poke the corners out. Insert the pillow form and tug the felt corners out if necessary. Here's the finished corner (photo 9).

Photo 9

# Collage Pillow

Use the pillow top as a blank canvas, adding graphic blocks of fabric and sparkling embellishments like sequins and beaded trim.

*The sum is greater than the parts.*

### EXPERIENCED BEGINNER

Cheat sheet for experienced beginner on page 49

## WHAT YOU NEED

Basic pillow-making tools & supplies

Approximately ½ yard of fabric for the front

Approximately ½ yard of fabric for the back and the band on the front

14 x 18-inch pillow form

Scraps of fabric in complementary colors

Vintage sequins

Approximately ¼ yard of vintage beaded trim

Contrasting thread

12-inch invisible zipper

## FINISHED SIZE

Approximately 14 x 18 inches

## HOW YOU MAKE IT

1 For the pillow front and back, cut one piece that's 15 x 19 inches from each of the fabrics.

2 Embellish the front of the pillow by adding squares of fabric, decorative stitching, and sequins. Have fun with this step! Play around with the decorations you want to add before you start stitching them in place (photo 1). Then, practice stitching with scraps, to be sure you're happy with your design elements (photo 2).

In this project, the two green squares were placed first and covered by the band that was cut to the width of the front of the pillow (19 inches). To apply the appliqués, use plenty of pins to keep them in place as you sew them on, using a zigzag or other decorative stitch as desired. (If your fabric allows, you could also use fusible web to secure the appliqués.) The strip of metallic organza was added next, and it was decorated with two vintage sequins. Finally, a length of vintage beaded trim was stitched on by hand, with a running stitch.

3 Install a zipper in the bottom seam of the pillow; we used an invisible zipper in this project. Remember to install the

Photo 1

Photo 2

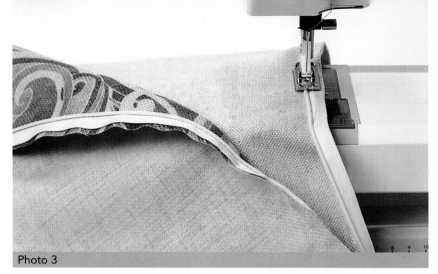

Photo 3

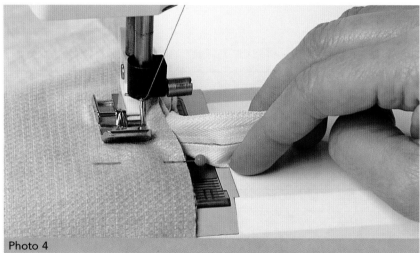

Photo 4

invisible zipper before any seams are sewn. The right sides of the zipper tape should face the right sides of the fabric, with the zipper teeth at the seamline. Stitch each side of the zipper tape, using the invisible zipper foot (photo 3). After installing the zipper, place the pillow front and back together, right sides facing, and use the regular zipper foot to finish the bottom seam, starting above the last few stitches of the zipper installation (photo 4).

4 Unzip the zipper. (If you don't unzip the zipper, you can't turn the pillow right side out!) With the right sides together, pin and stitch the remaining three seams around the pillow. Turn right side out through the opened zipper and stuff with the pillow form.

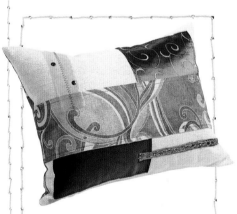

## Tip

This project was stitched with ⅝-inch seams, to create a nice plump pillow.

# *Edgy* Bolsters

*Liberate your seams by putting them on the outside of these funky bolsters. Add some ribbon embellishment to complement an unforgettable fabric.*

*Free your seams!*

**EXPERIENCED BEGINNER**

Cheat sheet for experienced beginner
  on page 49

# Big Loopy Bolster

## WHAT YOU NEED

Basic pillow-making tools & supplies

Approximately ⅝ yard of print fabric

7 x 18-inch pillow form

Thread to match the fabric and the trim

Various trims, such as vintage rayon seam binding, organza ribbon, and velvet ribbon

20-inch invisible zipper

## FINISHED SIZE

Approximately 7 x 18 inches

## HOW YOU MAKE IT

1 Cut one piece of fabric that's 19 x 23 inches, and cut two 8-inch circles for the ends. (You may want to measure around the circumference of your pillow form before you cut, as the fullness of some forms may vary. Just like us, I guess!)

2 Pin the cover on the pillow and determine the "front" (photo 1). Mark the areas that you'll embellish with the ribbon medallions. This fabric has circles in various sizes that are perfect to decorate.

3 Create the medallions from seam binding and organza ribbon; our seam binding was ½ inch wide, and the organza ribbon was ¾ inch wide. Begin with the seam binding: Cut lengths that are about 24 inches long, and press in half lengthwise. (The lengths of your ribbon may vary according to the motifs on your fabric.) Open the binding and use matching thread to backstitch it to the pillow in a lazy spiral, beginning in the center of the circular motif (photo 2). Follow the pressed center of the seam binding as you stitch, guiding the seam binding around the circle. Fold the binding back in on itself as you work.

Photo 1

Photo 2

To create the medallions with the wider organza ribbon, simply lay the ribbon around the motif and stitch in the center of the ribbon, using a running stitch. Pull the stitches slightly; it will fold in on itself as you work. The organza medallions in this project have two revolutions of ribbon around the motif.

Photo 3

4 Install a zipper in the seam of the pillow; we used an invisible zipper in this project. (Just because.) Remember to install the invisible zipper before any seams are sewn. The right sides of the zipper tape should face the right sides of the fabric, with the zipper teeth at the seamline. Stitch each side of the zipper tape, using the invisible zipper foot. After installing the zipper, place the pillow front and back together, right sides facing, and use the regular zipper foot to finish the seam, starting above the last few stitches of the zipper installation. Turn the pillow right side out.

5 Mark the four corners of each circular end (photo 3), as well as the decorated pillow. To mark the pillow, fold it in half with the seam at one side and mark the opposite side. Then, fold in the opposite direction, matching the markings, and mark the remaining sides.

Photo 4

6 Pin the ends to the pillow with the *wrong* sides together, beginning by matching the marks you made in step 5 (photo 4). Use lots of pins! (If you want to insert organza ribbon into the seam as we did, place 1½-inch wide ribbon between the pillow and the raw edges as you pin. Don't get too hung up on placing the ribbon a certain distance from the raw edges—we didn't.)

Stitch the ends to the bolster. You may need to ease one or the other side to fit, depending on how accurately you measured the pillow's circumference. To ease, use your fingers to spread the fabric as you stitch, gently pulling it taut as you stitch (photo 5). When you're done, you'll have a funky, organic ruffle at either end.

7 Insert the pillow form and check the fit, tweaking if necessary. Remove the pillow form and stitch the seams again for security. Leave the raw edges unfinished. Insert the pillow form through the zipper opening.

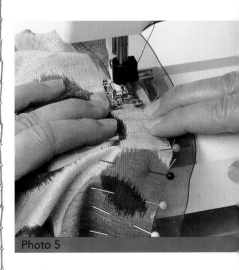

Photo 5

# Striped Bolster

## WHAT YOU NEED

Approximately ½ yard of print fabric

5 x 16-inch pillow form

Thread to match the fabric and the trim

Various trims, such as vintage rayon seam binding, organza ribbon, and velvet ribbon

Paper-backed fusible web tape (optional)

14-inch invisible zipper

## FINISHED SIZE

Approximately 5 x 16 inches

## HOW YOU MAKE IT

1 Cut a piece of fabric that's 17 x 19 inches, and cut two 6-inch circles for the ends. (You may want to measure around the circumference of your pillow form before you cut, as we suggested in step 1 of the Loopy Bolster.)

2 Cut pieces of trim to 19 inches and apply to the fabric as desired. We used paper-backed fusible web tape to apply the rayon seam binding and the velvet ribbon, and used decorative stitching to secure the organza ribbon (photo 6). Be sure to test your materials before you fuse; some types of ribbon may not survive the heat of the iron. Use decorative stitching for any trims that can't be fused. And don't hesitate to embellish the fused trim with stitching if the spirit moves you.

3 After decorating the pillow, complete it as in steps 4 through 7 of the Loopy Bolster. We added a line of zigzag stitching in the seam allowances at either end, as you see in photo 7.

Photo 6

Photo 7